The accuracy of telephone reference/information services in academic libraries

two studies

by Marcia J. Myers & Jassim M. Jirjees

The Scarecrow Press, Inc.
Metuchen, N.J., & London • 1983

Library of Congress Cataloging in Publication Data

Myers, Marcia J., 1941–
    The accuracy of telephone reference/information services in
academic libraries.

    Includes bibliographies and index.
    1. Reference services (Libraries)—Standards—Northeastern
States. 2. Reference services (Libraries)—Standards—Southeastern
States. 3. Libraries, University and college—Northeastern States.
4. Libraries, University and college—Southeastern States.
I. Jirjees, Jassim M. II. Title.
Z711.M93 1983   025.5'2777   82–10785
    ISBN 0–8108–1584–2

Copyright © 1983 by Marcia J. Myers
         and Jassim M. Jirjees
Manufactured in the United States of America

CONTENTS

Preface, by Ralph Blasingame, Jr.   iv

I: TELEPHONE REFERENCE/INFORMATION
     SERVICES IN ACADEMIC LIBRARIES IN
     THE SOUTHEAST   vii

     Appendices   111

     Notes   134

     Bibliography   139

II: TELEPHONE REFERENCE/INFORMATION
     SERVICES IN SELECTED NORTHEASTERN
     COLLEGE LIBRARIES   143

     Appendices   244

     Notes   257

     Bibliography   263

Index to Parts I and II   267

[iii]

FOREWORD

Ralph Blasingame, Jr.

A little more than ten years ago, I wrote a preface to Terry Crowley's and Tom Childers's studies of information service in public libraries.[1] At the time, I was concerned that the method of measuring the accuracy of replies by librarians to certain questions might be abused. As it happens, only one instance of abuse has come to my attention. The greater problem seems to have been that the method has been used so infrequently. Despite Lancaster's description of those studies as "the most important work on unobtrusive evaluation to date"[2] and aside from the flurry of interest caused at the time, rather few applications have been reported. Enough applications have been reported, however, to reinforce the utility of the method and to indicate that the rather disappointing performance recorded is common and not limited to responses only to telephone inquiries.

Part of my pleasure at having been given this opportunity to write a preface for the present work by Myers and Jirjees is quite personal. Marcia was one of the library trainees employed by the Pennsylvania State Library to attend library school and then work in public libraries there while I was State Librarian. I was chairman of Jassim's research committee while he designed and carried through his Ph. D. thesis, upon which his part of this volume is based. But part of the pleasure is in being able to comment on these two developments of the Crowley-Childers method of measurement. Here are the first extended studies in unobtrusive measurement of reference service applied to academic libraries. Together, they demonstrate that the method is applicable to academic libraries and that performance in those libraries is not far different from performance in public libraries. These studies also tend to confirm that

[iv]

improvement of reference service is probably not best sought through refinement of input standards of the traditional kinds. Reflection on the results of these studies, then, might profitably lead us to look in other directions. For one, it is now clear that unobtrusive testing of reference service can be carried out in public and academic libraries. In the latter, such testing can be carried out with assurance (always assuming respect for the method) in public and private academic libraries; in two-year and four-year colleges and in those offering some graduate programs. What is not clear is the extent to which librarians generally have set objectives (great or small) concerning their role(s) in giving reference service. Thus, the library manager who reads these two studies might have some broad issues in mind.

One of those issues centers on the model, or "ideal, " of performance we have before us. In reference service (and elsewhere in our work), we seem to believe that we can do everything anyone asks. We have, for lack of a better term, a "100% model. " I draw this conclusion from a variety of sources and experiences, but also from the lack of statements of policy that qualify that model. For example, objections to the earlier studies tended toward complaints about the methodology and even to suggestions of a failure to observe ethical standards, rather than to comments about unrealistic expectations or suggestions for inclusion in policy statements of some limitations. The present studies, then, added to the earlier ones, might best drive us toward consideration of basic elements in management.

And are we "in control" or "out of control"? We now have a variety of tools to enable us to be in control, in the sense of being reasonably sure that our decisions are actually reflected in appropriate actions. That the unobtrusive method demonstrated here has been so little used raises the question as to whether we really care to be in control of our institutions.

The present works may be read as evidence of technical developments of existing tools. But, more importantly, they raise much more basic issues of definition of purpose, of determination to manage for results, and, finally, of commitment to accountability.

Notes

1. Crowley, T., and T. Childers. Information Service in Public Libraries: Two Studies. Metuchen, N.J.: Scarecrow, 1971.

2. Lancaster, F. W. The Measurement and Evaluation of Library Services. Washington, D.C.: Information Resources, 1977, p.91.

Part I:

TELEPHONE REFERENCE/INFORMATION
SERVICES IN ACADEMIC LIBRARIES IN THE
SOUTHEAST

by
Marcia J. Myers

CONTENTS: PART I

Introduction   5

1. THE PROBLEM AND RELATED LITERATURE   7

2. RESEARCH QUESTIONS AND METHOD-
   OLOGY   14

3. FINDINGS: UNOBTRUSIVE MEASURES AND
   THE QUERIES   34

4. FINDINGS: LIBRARY CLASSIFICATIONS   61

5. FINDINGS: LIBRARY INDEPENDENT
   VARIABLES   71

6. FINDINGS: REFERENCE INDEPENDENT
   VARIABLES   82

7. SUMMARY, CONCLUSIONS, AND
   COMMENTS   103

Appendices

    A. Query response form   111
    B. Proxy instructions   112
    C. Survey of academic library reference /
       information services   116
    D. Distribution of performance on the
       dependent variables by type of institution
       and control   122
    E. Summary statistics on the performance
       score: number of correct responses by
       library classification   124
    F. Validity of the survey responses   127

G. Raw and rank order data on reference
volumes held, hours of service per
week, and number of correct responses
by library   130
H. Statistics describing reference volumes
held by type of institution   132
I. Statistics describing hours of reference
service per week by type of institution   133

Notes   134
Bibliography   139

LIST OF TABLES

1. Population and Sample of Academic
   Libraries in Nine Southeastern States by
   Type of Institution and Control   20

2. Number of Libraries Tested, Eliminated,
   and Analyzed by Type of Institution and
   Control   36

3. Percentage of Correct Responses by
   Query   43

4. Performance Distribution for the Minor
   Dependent Variables on Fourteen Queries
   by Accuracy of Response   56

5. Median Performance Scores by Type of
   Institution   64

6. Matrix of Probabilities on Number of
   Correct Responses by Type of Institution   65

7. Percentage Distribution of Performance on
   the Minor Dependent Variable: Source
   Volunteered by Accuracy of Response and
   Type of Institution   67

8. Matrix of Rank Order Correlations for
   Seven Library Independent Variables   73

9. Summary of Stepwise Multiple Regression
   Analysis with Seven Library Independent
   Variables for All Academic Libraries   75

[1]

10. Correlation Between the Number of Correct Responses and Seven Library Independent Variables for Four-Year Colleges Without Graduate Programs by Type of Control   77

11. Percentage Distribution of the Performance Score: Number of Correct Responses by Library Volumes Held in Selected Categories   79

12. Percentage Distribution of the Performance Score: Number of Correct Responses by Library Hours Per Week in Selected Categories   80

13. Rank Order Correlation Matrix for the "Developmental Guidelines" and Selected Variables   86-87

14. Rank Order Correlation Matrix for the Individual "Developmental Guidelines" Questions That Were Associated Significantly with the Number of Correct Responses   89

15. Matrix of Rank Order Correlations for the Major Dependent Variable and Independent Variables Concerning Library/Reference Hours of Service   92

16. Matrix of Rank Order Correlations for the Major Dependent Variable and Independent

[2]

Variables Concerning Library/Reference
Volumes Held   93

17. Summary of Stepwise Multiple Regression
Analysis with Library and Reference In-
dependent Variables for All Academic
Libraries   95

18. Percentage Distribution of the Performance
Score: Number of Correct Responses by
Reference Volumes Held in Selected
Categories   99

19. Percentage Distribution of the Performance
Score: Number of Correct Responses by
Reference Hours Per Week in Selected
Categories   101

[3]

INTRODUCTION

Librarians are faced with an increasing need to evaluate their services; reference work remains one of the more difficult areas to assess. The controversial national "Developmental Guidelines" for reference/information services do not suggest minimum levels of performance.[1] Consequently, we have progressed very little since 1964, when Rothstein noted:

> Evaluation presupposes measurement against a specific standard or yardstick or goal, and no area of library service has been more deficient in such standards than reference services.[2]

This book provides some insight into the effectiveness of reference/information services in academic libraries. The chief investigative technique used was nonreactive unobtrusive measurement, a method that does not influence or contaminate the objects being assessed. In this study, users' questions were simulated via telephone. This contrived situation permitted observation of the library staff's performance (or failure to perform) without their knowledge that they were being tested.

The performance of staff in the forty academic libraries in this investigation was considerably less than perfect. The findings of this study are offered to stimulate further research, aid the formation of standards for reference services, and ultimately lead to improvement in these services.

Only the salient details of a dissertation are reported here. Readers interested in a fuller treatment are urged to consult the original publication and other works based on that study.[3]

[5]

Many individuals have contributed to this work. Among those who should be thanked are the anonymous proxies and nameless reference librarians who provided much of the data. Special appreciation is extended to those who participated from pretest to publication, including colleagues at Florida State University and Miami-Dade Community College (especially Mary Malcolm, Peggy Patton, and Mildred Kirsner), members of my family (especially Madeline Dodd and Ruth Myers), and my research committee (Louis Bender, Ronald Blazek, Gerald Jahoda, and John Goudeau, major professor). The author gratefully and belatedly acknowledges the assistance of the late Gloria Jahoda and John Goudeau, who would have enjoyed reading this briefer version. The work herein is dedicated to these and to all individuals whose participation (both knowing and unknowing) made this study possible.

1.
THE PROBLEM AND RELATED LITERATURE

In his definitive survey of measurement and evaluation, Lancaster points out that the quality of reference service depends upon the quality of the collection and the ability of the library staff to exploit the collection effectively. He also notes that the quality of reference service must be judged in terms of how completely, accurately, and efficiently user demands are satisfied. [1]

Studies of reference services usually indicate that patrons are well pleased; user satisfaction is frequently above 80 or 90 percent. Librarians report that they are answering better than 90 percent of all questions; however, data from unobtrusive measurement studies indicate that there is reason to suspect these findings. [2]

Unobtrusive studies using contrived-observation, when the subjects were not aware that their performance on test reference questions was being observed, provide evidence that only about half of the reference questions are answered correctly. [3] In speculating on the reasons for nonreview of the sober findings of these studies, Martin points out:

> One possibility is that most librarians are convinced that their reference service is accurate and and thorough; but if this is the case, why not put it to the test? Another possibility is that librarians are uncertain about the success of their ministrations to users, and simply do not want to find out. [4]

One might add a third possibility to Martin's speculations: since these studies concerned public libraries, academic

[7]

librarians have ignored the results as not applicable to their situation. This investigation indirectly pursues this third possibility.

Significance of the Problem

At a time when library literature is replete with articles on computer and telecommunication advances, which appear ready to revolutionize reference and other library services, it seems appropriate to reexamine the informational aspect of traditional reference services. The effectiveness of these new services will perhaps be dependent upon the traditional reference/information techniques that are their foundation.

As Rothstein indicated in his seminal work, reference service has not always been a traditional library activity; however, by the end of the nineteenth century, personal assistance was characteristic of reference service in all types of libraries.[5] Although reference services have been studied in this century, no solution to the problem of obtaining meaningful evaluation data has emerged.

Hutchins, noting the difficulty of accurately evaluating the reference work of a given library, suggested a series of research studies in 1944.[6] Thirty years later, Katz wrote:

> There are good to excellent reference librarians
> and equally good to excellent reference services.
> Still if one believes a potentially excellent reference
> librarian is something more than an accident of
> birth, it would seem to some value to consider how
> to guide him.[7]

Related Research

The literature dealing with the effectiveness of reference/information services using unobtrusive measures in academic libraries is scant, compared with that available on public libraries. Selected research pertinent to this study is briefly summarized below. General literature on the evaluation and measurement of reference services has not been reviewed since it has been more than adequately covered elsewhere.[8]

Public library studies

The first major test of reference/information service performance using simulated patrons or proxies was conducted by Crowley in 1968. [9] In developing the unobtrusive measurement framework, Crowley used in-person and telephone fact-type queries in twelve medium-sized public libraries in New Jersey where the respondents were unaware of the testing. Data on correctness, incorrectness, or inability to provide answers were collected for ten queries. Sixty-five of the analyzed responses, or 54 percent, were considered correct. No significant difference was found in the proportion of questions correctly answered by the six libraries with high expenditures when compared with the six libraries with low expenditures.

Childers, the most active unobtrusive measurement researcher, first refined his contrived observation technique in his 1970 study. [10] He investigated the relationships between the correctness of the responses to twenty-six telephone requests of fact-type queries and various statistics describing twenty-five public libraries in New Jersey. Five response scales were correlated with the independent variables. "Scale A," which scored all responses that were not the correct answer as zero, was found to be the most discriminating scale. Fifty-five percent of the "Scale A" responses were correct.

The single independent variable that showed the highest correlation with the dependent variable was Hours Open. When twenty-seven independent variables were compared, expenditures for all personnel was the best indicator of the strength among the remaining twenty-six. Six other variables that best indicated the variation in the other independent variables were related to finances.

Peat, Marwick, Mitchell and Company [11] used both indepth and fact-type queries in their three-part survey of twenty public libraries of comparable size in California. Poor staff attitudes and actual incompetence were seen as frequent reasons for poor performance. The researchers concluded that people would not seek to meet their information needs when the expectation of success was so low.

It should be noted that a library that did well on one part of the three-part test was not any more likely to do well on the other parts of the test. The instrument used in this California study may have lacked internal reliability.

Weech perceived unobtrusive measures as the primary trend in reference evaluation in 1974. He observed:

> Whether this trend will continue will probably depend as much on the library profession's acceptance of the technique as a legitimate and appropriate one as on any other factor.[12]

The use of unobtrusive measurement as an ethical research method has been questioned and countered by Childers, who pointed out that the librarians were being tested only in their public capacities without sacrificing separate privacies.[13]

Powell[14] chose obtrusive rather than unobtrusive measurement, but not for ethical reasons. He felt that the librarians' motivation would be more likely to be equal and constant if they knew that they were being tested. Additionally, the obtrusive technique allowed for followup analysis to isolate the sources used by the librarians in fifty-one Illinois public libraries to answer the twenty-five reference queries.

Powell found that the participants answered approximately 59 percent of the test questions correctly. When sources owned were considered, the questions that participants possibly could have answered and actually answered correctly rose to a mean of 78 percent.

Multiple regression analysis indicated that there was a significant, causal relationship between the reference collection size and the percentage of test questions answered correctly. Additionally, the relationship between the two variables was found to be nonlinear. Diminishing returns were noticeable once a reference collection size of approximately 3,500 volumes was reached. The weaker relationship between the reference collection size and the "percent of possible actually answered correctly," also nonlinear, was viewed as possibly more influenced by the skill of the reference librarian.

The majority of the public library studies reported here were well conceived and well executed; however, it was not clear if their findings would be applicable to academic libraries. In his review of the jointly published work of Crowley and Childers, Haro indicated that their work in unobtrusive measurement had serious and important implications for academic libraries as well.[15] Unfortunately, these implications had not been adequately tested.

Academic library studies

Only two prior research studies were identified that involved unobtrusive measures of academic libraries. The better of these was a pilot study conducted at the University of Minnesota Libraries in 1973.[16] King and Berry attempted to evaluate the accuracy of responses to questions asked via telephone, the level of interviewing by the staff person, and the attitude of the staff person as perceived by the proxy user.

The percentages of correct answers by the library divisions ranged from 40 to 90 percent. At times during the study, it was found that the proxy's rating of staff pleasantness was as important as the correct answer in determining if the proxy would call that information source again. Other trends found by the researchers were that interviewing of the caller was not practiced where it might have helped the library staff member locate a correct answer, and that the source of the answer was seldom given to the user.

Unobtrusive measures may not have been used in a pure form in the King and Berry study. Prior to the beginning of the test, the various divisions submitted sample questions of the type that they were frequently asked to answer. Since the divisions submitted questions, they would have been aware that they were to be studied even though the exact time, date, or questions were not known. The type of test questions asked, coupled with the staff's probable knowledge of a testing situation, may account for the higher percentage of correct answers in this study as compared with other research using unobtrusive measures.

The second published study of academic library reference service involving unobtrusive measures was a 1972 survey sponsored by the state of Ohio.[17] A 10-percent sample of public and academic libraries was to have been used; however, many libraries were not open during the time that the calls were placed. Two fact-type queries were asked via telephone between 8 a.m. and 2 p.m. on a Saturday.

Responses were rated as correct, incorrect, or unable to give an answer. All nine of the academic library answers were correct. Of the twenty-nine public library answers, only twenty-five answers, or 86 percent, were correct. Based on the limited data available, one is tempted to conclude that academic libraries out-perform public libraries in Ohio. No conclusions were drawn by the researchers.

The King and Berry research and the Ohio report were the only research studies located by this investigator dealing with unobtrusive measurement of academic libraries. There were, however, some additional studies of reference services pertaining to academic libraries that were pertinent to this research.

In a project commissioned by the Reference Standards Committee, selected school, special, academic, and public libraries were used to gather information for the purpose of developing library reference service standards.[18] A group of ten graduate students were selected to conduct the project, which became a learning experience for them. This research format would explain why the methodology lacked rigor.

The study suggested uniform qualitative standards for all types of libraries with a self-evaluation process that should include a thorough use study. It was also recommended that the Reference Standards Committee include some quantitative standards, such as the size of the collection, space per patron, and hours per week of service.

Billy Wilkinson and A. Venable Lawson separately examined reference services using a case study approach at Columbia University in 1971.[19] Wilkinson investigated reference services in the undergraduate and main libraries at two universities and two liberal arts college libraries.

He concluded that the university undergraduate librarians at Michigan and Cornell offered low-caliber reference services and had failed to close the gap between class instruction and library services. In contrast, the services offered for undergraduates at Earlham College, particularly the library instruction program and the less passive individual reference assistance, should serve as archetypes worthy of imitation. Among Wilkinson's suggestions for further research was the need for an unobtrusive measurement study of academic libraries.

Lawson conducted a case study of the reference services at the Emory University and the University of Florida libraries. He concluded that before standards could be considered, the role of university reference service needed more careful definition. The question requiring resolution was whether the role of reference librarians is to instruct the user in effective library use, to guide the user to needed information and resources, or to supply the information and resources without instruction and guidance.

This problem of role definition was later studied by Duncan[20] using eighteen university librarians and nineteen college reference librarians. University reference personnel thought reference work was more bibliographic than the college respondents, who provided a wider range of services. The college respondents also indicated that their departments leaned more toward the moderate-to-maximum philosophy of reference services. Duncan recommended that there be written definitive job descriptions and statements of philosophy and objectives.

The suggestions, problems, and the investigative techniques reported in the literature were used to formulate four research questions for this study. These research questions are detailed in the next chapter.

2.
RESEARCH QUESTIONS AND METHODOLOGY

This chapter details the four research questions; the general research design of the study; and the methodology and procedures used to select the sample libraries; develop, pretest, and apply the instruments; and treat the data collected. The assumptions and limitations of the study, which pertain primarily to the population and the investigative technique, are presented at the end of the chapter.

Research Questions

Since the objective of this study was to explore the effectiveness of reference/information services in academic libraries using unobtrusive measurement, research questions are offered rather than formal hypotheses. The four major questions addressed by this investigation are as follows:

1. Can reference/information services in academic libraries be unobtrusively measured by performance on fact-type queries asked via telephone?

2. Are there differences in effectiveness among academic libraries classified as to type of control and/or type of institution?

3. Is there a direct relationship between the number of correct responses and certain descriptive statistics collected by the National Center for Education Statistics,[1] such as total operating expenditures or number of volumes in the library collection, that explains the differences among academic libraries?

[14]

4. Is there a direct relationship between the number of correct responses and selected reference policies, procedures, and statistics, such as compliance with the "Developmental Guidelines," referral of unanswered reference questions to a senior staff member, or number of volumes in the reference collection, that explains the differences among academic libraries?

Definitions

While common terminology is used throughout this study, definitions are offered to clarify terms in the research questions.

Reference/information services. That aspect of traditional library reference services with the object of providing the information itself rather than instruction and guidance in the pursuit of information is referred to as reference/information services throughout this study.

Unobtrusive measures. Observations collected without distortions due to the assessment process itself are unobtrusive measures. In this study, the nonreactive measurement situation consisted of published records and fact-type queries applied via telephone. The latter simulated field conditions so that library staff members would not be aware that they were being tested.

Fact-type queries. Reference questions that usually do not require negotiation and can be satisfied by a predetermined short answer are fact-type queries.

Performance. Selected actions by library staff members on each fact-type query constituted performance or the dependent variables in this study. The major performance variable observed was accuracy of response. Other aspects of performance related to telephone reference/information services were also studied, such as the number of times the responding library staff member volunteered the source used. A performance score for each of the eight dependent variables on all fact-type queries was arrived at by summing the performance on each query.

Effectiveness. As used in this study, the term "effectiveness" may refer to performance on the major dependent

variable alone, which is the accuracy of the responses to the
fact-type queries; or it may refer to the performance score
on a minor dependent variable controlled by the major dependent variable; e.g., if the response was correct, the number
of times at least one call back was required.

Academic libraries. Academic libraries are those institutions listed in Library Statistics of Colleges and Universities that have been further defined as to type of control
and/or type of institution. Academic libraries have been
categorized into three major classifications as follows:
(1) type of control--public or private; (2) type of institu-
tion--two-year colleges, four-year colleges without graduate
programs, four-year colleges with graduate programs, or
universities; and (3) type of institution and control--public
and private two-year colleges, public and private four-year
colleges without graduate programs, public and private four-
year colleges with graduate programs, or public and private
universities. To conserve space in table presentations, the
types of institutions will be abbreviated as follows: two-yr.,
four-N, four-G., or univ.

Research Design

The general research method is viewed as descriptive,
since existing conditions are surveyed and the findings presented for other investigators to pursue under more controlled
experimental conditions. In 1974, Weech observed:

Until such a time as there are guidelines for gathering and measuring data, evaluation of reference
service is likely to continue to be exploratory and
indeterminant. [2]

Since evaluation guidelines do not presently exist, this is an
exploratory study; its findings may assist in the formation of
such guidelines.

Selection of Libraries

Population

Because of the investigator's research interest in the
area, academic libraries in nine contiguous southeastern states
were selected as the population for this study. After the sam-

ple was drawn, it became apparent that certain institutions within the finite population might be recognized. For reasons of confidentiality, the states are not specifically named. It does not compromise anonymity, however, to reveal that the forty libraries that were subjected to final analysis were all located in institutions accredited by the Southern Association of Colleges and Schools.

When the population for this study was drawn in December 1976, the 1973 Library Statistics of Colleges and Universities had been published but the more recent data from 1975 were only available on magnetic tape. The data collected by the National Center for Education Statistics in the 1975 Library General Information Survey (LIBGIS) were accessed via EDSTAT II to draw the population for this study using keyed components that identified state, type of control, and type of institution. In a manner similar to that used for academic library statistics in the printed version, the staff at the National Center for Education Statistics classified libraries by type of control and type of institution. The investigator then manually scrutinized the printouts provided, placed limitations on the population, and drew the sample.

Limitations on the population. Since academic libraries were operationally defined as libraries listed in Library Statistics of Colleges and Universities, institutions that did not complete the Library General Information Survey (LIBGIS) questionnaire for 1975 were automatically eliminated from the population under study.

Specialty schools, libraries with fewer than two staff members with graduate degrees, and institutions that had predominantly black student bodies were eliminated from the sample. These restrictions were added to the population to eliminate variables that the investigator could not control and that were outside the main interest of the study. These restrictions also reduce the chance that library staff members would become suspicious of being tested, refuse to answer queries, or perform in other unnatural ways.

It was felt that if a test query outside the appropriate subject area were asked in a medical school, theological seminary, or other specialty institution, it would fail to provide a true indication of that library's performance and increase the likelihood of the test itself being discovered. The nonreactivity of the instrument could most easily be maintained by asking queries that were not atypical for most academic libraries.

Additionally, the same queries should be asked in each institution to test for differences; therefore, it was more logical to drop all specialty institutions from the population. Forty-seven limited-offering institutions were eliminated from the population. These included medical schools, schools of law, theological seminaries, and other specialty schools.

In his study, Childers experienced reactivity or exposure and conjectured that his test reference questions obtruded first and most easily in the public libraries with smaller total expenditures where there were fewer library staff members to handle the question.[3] It seemed logical that the more staff members with graduate degrees the more likely the unobtrusiveness of the instrument could be maintained; a further limitation was therefore placed on the population for this study by selecting only academic libraries employing at least two staff members with graduate degrees. One hundred institutions did not qualify on this criterion.

While the influence of race and sex on reference performance is not known, the investigator had some control over these variables through employment of proxies and through limitations on the population. In consultation with the Research Committee, it was decided to eliminate all institutions that had a predominantly black student body and employ white proxies, who had no identifiable accent, of the sex appropriate to the sex of the student body of the institutions in the sample. Fifty-one institutions met this criterion and were removed from the population.

Sample

After the elimination process, 361 institutions remained in the population. These institutions were numbered consecutively within each of the eight subsets or strata. Next, a table of random numbers was used to draw a random sample, without replacement, from each of the strata.

Stratified random samples may be used when the objective is to reduce sampling error, to lower the cost of a study, or to make comparisons among various subpopulations. Since the primary purpose of this study was to test differences in effectiveness of reference/information services among classifications of academic libraries, a stratified random sample was appropriate.

Stratified samples can also be used as a means of controlling relevant variables. While the actual proportion of the various classifications of the libraries in the population was known, a disproportionate stratified sample was purposefully drawn to make the strata equal in size for comparison purposes. As Kish explains, if the strata are also the domains or subpopulations of study then equal allocation benefits their estimates and comparisons.[4]

The size of the smallest stratum, five private university libraries, was used to fix the sample size for all strata. When possible, the strata were oversampled to allow for alternates.

Table 1 details the number of libraries in the population and the percentage of the population actually sampled. The percentages, based on the five sampled libraries subjected to analysis, ranged from a little over 3 percent to 100 percent. The forty libraries sampled represent an 11-percent sample of the finite population of 361 academic libraries in the Southeast.

An estimating formula was used along with statistics computed from the 870 observations collected in previous studies to test the adequacy of the sample size proposed for this research. The tests indicated that the sample would be adequate for an exploratory study. The exact precision of the stratified sample in this study was computed after the performance test and is detailed in Chapter 3.

Instruments and Data Collection

Instruments in this study included observations on fact-type queries asked via telephone, variables selected from the National Center for Education Statistics 1975 LIBGIS data, and a questionnaire constructed by the investigator to collect independent variables related to reference policies, procedures, and statistics. The design and application of each of the three instruments are briefly described below.

Queries and the dependent variables

Actual queries or close simulations of real queries were selected from previous studies and from a Query Bank

Table 1

POPULATION AND SAMPLE OF ACADEMIC LIBRARIES
IN NINE SOUTHEASTERN STATES BY TYPE
OF INSTITUTION AND CONTROL

Type of Institution and Control	Number in Southeast	Percent of Stratum Sampled
Two-Year Colleges		
Public	148	3.4%
Private	12	41.7
Four-Year Without Graduate Programs		
Public	13	38.5
Private	76	6.6
Four-Year with Graduate Programs		
Public	60	8.3
Private	30	16.7
Universities		
Public	17	29.4
Private	5	100.0
Totals	361	11.1%

NOTE: Includes only libraries that completed the 1975 LIBGIS questionnaire, had more than partial data in the EDSTAT II data file, were not specialty institutions, had at least two FTE library staff with a graduate degree, and did not have predominantly black student bodies.

established by Gerald Jahoda to develop a Tool Descriptor Matrix.5

The Matrix, designed as an aid in the selection of answer-providing tools, was originally tested and revised using 435 queries and suggestions from twenty-three reference librarians in university science and technology libraries. It was subsequently tested and revised using approximately 2,000 queries from public libraries.

Twenty-three queries, query revisions, and query rationales were pretested in institutions similar to, but not among, those that would be drawn in the sample. The pretest was conducted from December 1976 through February 1977 by twenty-three separate pretesters. Sixty-eight institutions, located in sixteen states, were used to collect 123 observations.

Rationales were also tested for each query to assist in simulating real queries and controlling the amount of explanatory information. The accompanying rationale was given with every application of the query.

As a result of the pretest, fourteen queries were selected for the actual study, instructions for the proxies were revised, the timing for the application of the queries was extended to avoid exposure or awareness of the test in the smaller academic libraries, and the scale for scoring the correctness of the response was simplified.

Test queries and rationales. The fourteen queries and the accompanying rationales selected for this study are as follows:

1. Who was Secretary of State when Sumner Welles was his assistant? (I know it was during Franklin Roosevelt's administration.)

2. What is the symbol for a population mean? (If asked, you may say: my English instructor mentioned it in class and I'd like to use it in an essay I'm writing on symbolism.)

3. What are the names of the books that make up Lawrence Durrell's Alexandrian tetralogy? (The book I'm looking in mentions them but not their titles and I'm writing a paper and need to know.)

4. Who said something like: the naive and the beautiful have no enemy but time? (It's just perfect for a paper I'm writing, some famous American or British author said it and I know it isn't new.)

5. When was George Washington given the title of General of the Armies of the United States? (I'm giving a speech and I need to know.)

6. Who is the president of the American Society for Information Science? (I'm writing a letter and need to know.)

7. What is the Zip Code for Behrend College in Erie, Pennsylvania? (I'm writing a letter and need to know.)

8. When did China orbit its first satellite? (If asked, you may say: I want to use the date as an example of China's late start in the space race in a paper I'm writing.)

9. Is the book Albert Einstein and the Cosmic World Order, by Cornelius Lanczos, recommended for laymen? (If asked, you may say: I want to read something I can understand about Einstein's work and this particular book was recommended to me.)

10. What is the address of Mexico City College? (Someone in one of my classes told me it is a very good school and has recently become a university.)

11. Who is the President of the American Library Association? (I'm writing a paper on older professional associations and need to know.)

12. Who were the stars in the 1960 Broadway production of Camelot? (For a paper I'm doing I need the names of the actors who played Arthur, Lancelot, and Guinevere.)

13. Where is the nearest airport to Warren, Pennsylvania? (My airline keeps saying I can take a bus from Pittsburgh and I know there must be a closer airport in northwest Pennsylvania.)

14. Who said: "There are two good things in life, freedom of thought and freedom of action"? (I know that's an exact quotation but I don't have the author's name.)

No query was chosen for the actual study that had not been partially answered or completely answered by at least one of the four types of institutions: two-year colleges, four-year colleges without graduate programs, four-year colleges with graduate programs, and universities. In general, the queries chosen fell in the 25-75 percentile range. This range was selected because differences in effectiveness of telephone reference services would be more easily detected if staff members were unlikely to obtain all correct or all incorrect answers.

The sources needed to answer each query selected for the actual study were checked against reference standard lists. In general, all queries could be answered with reference sources normally accessible to academic libraries. Queries 4, 10, and 14 were more dependent upon ownership of a particular title than the other queries; therefore, two additional queries on holdings were selected for application after the performance test as follows:

A. Does the library have the 12th, 13th, and/or 14th editions of John Bartlett's Familiar Quotations? (If asked, you may say: I need several quotations for a paper I want to write and know this is a good source.)

B. Do you have a recent edition of World of Learning? (If asked, you may say: I am interested in finding out if the library owns the book and if so, which is the most recent edition owned.)

Query A is related to queries 4 and 14 and query B is related to query 10.

Data collection. It was likely that busy and slack times for the library staff, as well as difference in staff members themselves, might influence the dependent variable. To minimize the effect of these factors, the queries were randomized for each institution as to day of week and time of day within dates and times the institution was open for a normal academic term. The college and university catalogs for all institutions in the sample were examined for term beginning and ending dates, official holidays, and other events, such as days of required chapel for all students.

Half-hour intervals between 9 a.m. and 3:30 p.m. were selected as the time for the initial contacts, since all types of academic libraries were likely to be open for full service during these hours. All telephone calls were made Mondays through Fridays during the normal academic term for each institution.

Statistical tests conducted after the performance test was concluded indicated that the order of initial contact was random.

Since the college catalogs revealed that some of the sample institutions were not in full session during the summer months, the performance test was divided in half. Queries 1 through 7 were telephoned at the rate of one query every other week beginning February 21, 1977, and ending May 20, 1977. Queries 8 through 14 were called every other week beginning September 12, 1977, and ending December 9, 1977. The two queries dealing with holding information, queries A and B, were telephoned in January 1978.

The queries were asked in the same order at each library during approximately the same week. While the one-year data collection period may have introduced some bias, any contaminations were probably offset by a longer period between queries. As revealed in the pretest, many sample academic libraries would probably have become aware of a testing situation if the queries had been asked at more frequent intervals.

Since all institutions in the sample and their alternates had either a coed or female student body, only female proxies were employed. All twelve proxies were white; most were college students or homemakers. One proxy called both queries 3 and 11; the investigator asked queries 1 and 13. The proxy for each query telephoned all sample libraries and their alternates at random intervals assigned by the investigator.

The Query Response Form used to collect the dependent variables in this study is given in Appendix A. If asked, each proxy indicated that she was a student at the institution and gave a name designated by the investigator that would not reveal race or religion. In most cases, proxies used their

real names. Each proxy was given an excuse to use in the
event the library staff member wanted to call her back. For
example, the preassigned excuse for query 4 was as follows:
"I'm using a friend's phone but I can call you back later.
Should I ask for anyone special?"

Appendix B presents the detailed proxy instructions.
In addition to these written instructions, each proxy was
given a rehearsal on recording information on the Query
Response Form using data from the pretest.

Because of exposure problems encountered by Childers
in his study and in the pretest for this study, care was taken
to ensure a nonreactive instrument for this investigation by:
including only libraries with at least two staff members with
graduate degrees; choosing a large geographical sample area,
which made it unlikely that libraries were using the same
reference referral network, if any; selecting queries that
were not atypical of actual queries received in academic libraries; and applying the queries during the times and dates
when the libraries were open for full service and thus unlikely to notice the test. Despite these precautions, there
were instances where the test was noticed. Only those responses received in a nonreactive manner were used in the
final statistical analysis. The replacement of libraries with
their alternates is discussed in Chapter 2 along with observations on the applicability of unobtrusive measures to academic
libraries.

As indicated on the Query Response Form (see Appendix B), independent variables that could not be controlled were
collected so that their influence on the major dependent variable, if any, could be ascertained. The sex of the staff member responding, the day of the week and the time of day of
the initial telephone contact on that query, and the state in
which the institution was located were among these peripheral
independent variables. Since unobtrusive measurements have
not been applied to academic libraries on a large scale, this
study also examined the technique and its applicability to academic libraries.

Library independent variables

The seventy-six independent variables selected from
the Fall 1975 Library General Information Survey (LIBGIS) for
analysis in this study included absolute statistics (total expend-

itures) and tangenerated statistics, such as Librarians as a
Percent of Total Library Staff. The library independent variables are as follows: (1) volumes added; (2) volumes held;
(3) document volumes held; (4) microform book titles added;
(5) microform book titles held; (6) microform periodical titles
added; (7) microform periodical titles held; (8) other microforms added; (9) other microforms held; (10) motion pictures
added; (11) motion pictures held; (12) recordings added;
(13) recordings held; (14) filmstrips added; (15) filmstrips
held; (16) slides added; (17) slides held; (18) maps added;
(19) maps held; (20) other AV added; (21) other AV held;
(22) periodical titles; (23) chief librarians, FTE number;
(24) chief librarians, FTE salary; (25) assistant chief librarians, FTE number; (26) assistant chief librarians, FTE
salary; (27) all other librarians, FTE number; (28) all other
librarians, FTE salary; (29) media specialists, FTE number; (30) media specialists, FTE salary; (31) other professional staff, FTE number; (32) other professional staff, FTE
salary; (33) support staff, FTE number; (34) support staff,
FTE salary; (35) total staff, FTE number; (36) total staff,
FTE salary; (37) contributed services staff, FTE number;
(38) contributed service staff, FTE salary; (39) professional
staff, FTE number; (40) male professional staff, FTE number; (41) female professional staff, FTE number; (42) professional staff with less than bachelor's degree, FTE number; (43) professional staff with bachelor's degree, FTE number; (44) professional staff with graduate degree, FTE number;
(45) professional staff with graduate degree in library science, FTE number; (46) student assistance, number of hours;
(47) salaries and wages of library staff; (48) fringe benefit
expenditures; (49) wages of student assistance charged to
the library; (50) book expenditures; (51) periodical expenditures; (52) microform expenditures; (53) AV expenditures;
(54) binding expenditures; (55) equipment expenditures; (56) all
other expenditures; (57) total expenditures; (58) materials
circulated; (59) interlibrary loans provided; (60) interlibrary
loans received; (61) net assignable area; (62) shelving capacity; (63) seating capacity; (64) total hours open per week;
(65) total days open two hours or more; (66) participant in
consortium, etc.; (67) FTE students; (68) expenditures/FTE
students; (69) expenditures/full-time faculty; (70) expenditures
as % of institution budget; (71) volumes/FTE students;
(72) titles/FTE students; (73) FTE students/librarian;
(74) FTE students/other professional staff; (75) FTE students/
support staff; (76) librarians as % of total library staff.

Reference independent variables

If differences in effectiveness of telephone reference/
information services were found to exist among academic libraries, it would be of interest to relate these differences
to variables concerned with total library operations and also
to variables concerned with reference per se. Since variables pertaining to reference policies, procedures, and statistics are not easily available, a questionnaire was constructed
by the investigator to collect this data.

Design and pretest. Existing literature and the opinions of experts were used to select independent variables
pertinent to the effectiveness of reference/information services. The responses and comments from eighteen individuals
with expertise in reference/information services in academic
libraries were used to improve the final instrument, which
is presented in Appendix C.

Questions 1 through 30 were taken from the "Developmental Guidelines" with slight rephrasing to adapt them to
the five-option response scale. Guidelines 1.2, 1.9, and 2.1
were each formed into two questions. They are represented
by questions 2 and 3, 10 and 11, and 12 and 13, respectively,
on the questionnaire.

Questions 31 through 44 were designed to collect general information on reference procedures that might be related to performance on fact-type queries asked via telephone.
Statistics pertinent to reference/information services were
requested in questions 45 through 55. The remaining questions, 56 through 60, pertain to the survey respondent. These
questions were included to collect background information primarily for descriptive purposes.

Data collection. Names of the individuals responsible
for the delivery of reference/information services in the sample academic libraries and their alternates were located using
standard reference sources and current journals. When no
one individual was clearly identifiable as directly responsible
for reference/information services, the name of the assistant
librarian or head librarian was selected.

By January 1978, the proxies had completed telephoning
fourteen test queries and two holdings questions to fifty-nine
libraries. The survey was not mailed to these libraries until

April 6, 1978; thus no contamination of the performance test occurred.

Fifty-six questionnaires, or 94.9 percent, were returned. One completed questionnaire was received too late to be included in the data analysis. The fifty-five questionnaires analyzed represented 93.2 percent of the libraries surveyed.

Thirty-three libraries, or 58.9 percent of the fifty-six respondents, returned the questionnaire without receiving the followup letter, which was mailed on April 24th. Sixteen respondents (28.6 percent) returned the completed survey after the followup letter; seven (12.5 percent) completed the questionnaire after receiving a followup phone call from the investigator on May 3, 1978.

Treatment of the Data

Responses

All queries tested for this study had predetermined short answers. Queries with equivocal answers or other ambiguities were eliminated after the pretest. The pretest data also revealed that there was some disagreement on the ranking of responses for incorrect answers, partially correct answers, queries attempted but no answer found, and queries not attempted.

To increase objectivity, it was decided that in the actual study the responses on the dependent variables should be scored on a simple dichotomous scale, if applicable; a dichotomous scale was not used for the minor dependent variable "time."

The following dependent variables were observed: correct responses, response refusals, call backs, referrals, responses made immediately without a call back being required, responses attempted immediately and then a call back suggested, and the responses on which a source was volunteered.

On the major dependent variable, no credit was given for knowing the correct source but not providing the information requested. Referrals within the library or the parent institution were called and scored in order that decentralized reference services would not receive a biased rating compared with centralized reference services. While no points were given for queries not attempted, these nonattempts were tracked separately to investigate which type of queries and/or libraries had more refusals to answer.

A response refusal occurred when the proxy observed that the library staff member did not leave the telephone, did not consult a printed source or another library staff member, or did not suggest a referral. If the proxy was told to consult a publication, a person, or an organization by the library staff member, it was recorded as a referral; if the staff member answered from personal knowledge or made vague references to such sources as "an encyclopedia," this was recorded by the proxy but not counted as a source volunteered by the investigator.

A performance score concerning the total time required was computed to gain some insight into the relative efficiency by classifications of the academic libraries. The minor dependent variable "time" was created by summing the length of time (in seconds) on the responses attempted immediately, the length of time (in seconds) on the responses attempted immediately before suggesting a call back, and the total number of call backs required weighted by fifteen minutes (900 seconds).

Effectiveness was explored by controlling the minor dependent variables by the major dependent variable. While performance without a correct response being received is reported, the investigator considered the minor dependent variables of lesser interest.

A five-point scale was used in all appropriate questions in the survey of reference services. As Hill and Kerber indicate:

> Data-gathering instruments must not only be reliable, valid, and objective but must have discriminative power if the research demands predictions and/ or inferences of difference, magnitude, and relationship. [6]

So that any existing differences among libraries could be detected, discriminative power was maximized by choosing a five-point response scale that was long enough to measure the variable adequately.

Since the seventy-six library independent variables were gathered by the National Center for Education Statistics, the investigator's data treatment was confined to coding activities.

Coding

All responses to each query were considered as a group. Usually, the responses ranged from correct answers, based on the most current and authoritative source, to unwillingness or inability to find an answer at all. Correct answers were coded "1." All other responses on the major dependent variable were considered not correct and coded "0." After a lapse of several months, the responses were sorted by library and coded again by the investigator. The results were the same. Similar but less rigorous cross-checking was done with the minor dependent variables.

All coding sheets were sight-checked and the keypunched cards were verified. Ranges were checked for the minor dependent and peripheral variables using the computer. A few errors in sex of respondent, day of week, and time of day of initial telephone contact, caused by coding response set, were located and corrected prior to the data analysis. Additionally, the major dependent variable was listed for each library for each of the fourteen queries and checked against the original coding sheets.

The survey responses and the library independent variables were coded and sight-verified by the investigator after a one-week interval. The coding sheets were keypunched and verified by staff in the Miami-Dade Community College North Campus Computer Center. When the investigator checked the ranges of the punched data using the computer, minor errors were found and corrected.

Validity, reliability, and objectivity

Care was taken to ensure that the data collected by the constructed instruments measured consistently what they were intended to measure. The test queries were selected from actual queries or close simulation of actual queries. The instruments were reviewed by experts during the pretest for face validity. Queries and questionnaire items with ambiguities were eliminated, and scoring of the queries as to correctness was simplified.

Every effort was made to choose queries that would appear reasonable to an academic library staff member, so that a nonreactive instrument would be ensured. The instruments were objective in that acceptable answers were either predetermined, closed-option choice, or open-ended factual responses. Thus, the data were capable of consistent evaluation by more than one individual.

Recognizing that reliability is a necessary but insufficient condition for validity, the investigator performed certain reliability statistical tests after the observations in this study were collected. These tests are discussed along with presentation responses and data reductions in later chapters. While the comparisons do give some indication of the concurrent validity of the statistics as they pertain to fact-type queries, it was not the primary purpose of this study to investigate the validity of the "Developmental Guidelines" and statistics of library operations and reference services.

Statistical tests

Since many of the assumptions for the parametric statistics may not have been met, nonparametric statistics were used whenever possible in this study. For certain multivariate parametric procedures, there were no nonparametric alternatives and the parametric test was used. As pointed out by Blalock:

> Rather than using a weak or theoretically unsatisfactory nonparametric alternative, it would seem preferable in these instances to rely most heavily on the parametric procedures with the full recognition that the definitive results may not be attainable. [7]

When parametric tests were used in multivariate analysis, rank order correlations rather than product-moment correlations were calculated.

The nonparametric statistics used were of two main types: those that measure location and those that measure association. Location parameters or medians are measured to determine whether the independent groups come from the same population. Association measures indicate whether the two variables are independent or not. In addition, if they are related, some indication of the strength of the relationship may also be obtained. Tests such as the chi-square, the Kruskal-Wallis one-way analysis of variance by ranks, and the Spearman rank correlation coefficient were used. These tests and their assumptions are described in most standard textbooks.[8]

All computations were performed with the assistance of Miami-Dade Community College's IBM 370 computer, which the investigator accessed using the Statistical Package for Social Sciences.[9] A .05 probability level was chosen for all tests; however, results are displayed to the .10 level of significance in most instances.

Assumptions and Limitations

During this investigation, it was assumed that:

1. Telephone reference/information services are an important component of reference/information services in academic libraries and the library staff members will therefore attempt to give valid and reliable responses.

2. The responses given by an individual library staff member to the fact-type queries selected for this study are a legitimate indication of the overall effectiveness of telephone reference/information services in that academic library.

3. The data selected from the Library Statistics of Colleges and Universities are reliable, valid, and accurate; any errors and inconsistencies in these statistics will be normally distributed throughout the library independent variables in this study.

4. The instrument constructed to collect the reference independent variables is appropriate; the questions were answered honestly and accurately by the respondents.

All of the assumptions are by necessity, limitations of this study. Further major limitations pertain to the population and the methodology as follows:

1. The population was limited to academic libraries in nine southeastern states with several additional constraints; therefore, the results of this study

may not be generalizable to other academic libraries in other areas.

2. The chief investigative technique, unobtrusive
   measures, prevented observation on certain variables that may have a more direct influence on
   effectiveness of reference services. For example, no distinction could be made between professional and nonprofessional staff members responding on the dependent variable or between independent variables for multioutlet libraries.

3. Only fact-type queries were used in this study,
   and the results may not be generalizable to other
   aspects of reference services.

3.

FINDINGS: UNOBTRUSIVE MEASURES
AND THE QUERIES

Prior to this investigation, unobtrusive measures had
not been used in a major study of academic libraries. Additionally, this study covered a larger geographic area and applied test queries over a longer time span than other unobtrusive studies. Since the applicability of the unobtrusive
technique in this study was of interest to future researchers,
the first research question posed was:

Can reference/information services in academic libraries be unobtrusively measured by performance
on fact-type queries asked via telephone?

This chapter presents findings on unobtrusive measures and
the fact-type queries that are related to this research question. The last section of this chapter discusses the adequacy of the performance test and the sample size.

Unobtrusive Measures

Unobtrusive measures have several advantages over
other methods of observation. They are nonreactive, and
bias is reduced because the subjects are not aware that they
are being tested. Furthermore, unobtrusive measures do
not require the cooperation of the subjects.

As indicated by Webb and confirmed by Childers, the
primary disadvantage of the contrived observation type of unobtrusive measurement is the danger of being "caught."[1]
Once exposure took place in this study, the instrument was
considered reactive. To retain nonreactivity, the primary

[34]

strength of unobtrusive measures, exposed libraries were eliminated and replaced by nonexposed alternates. The replacement of libraries by their alternates will be briefly described, followed by an informal summarization of problems encountered with the unobtrusive measurement technique.

Replacement

Based on the pretest for this investigation and observations made by Childers on the delicacy of the technique, it was anticipated that the unobtrusive measures used in this study could become reactive. When a library staff member reacted in an unnatural manner, telephone calls were still continued to that library since it was possible that this was a one-time reaction unrelated to the performance test. When the pattern of responses indicated to the Research Committee that the library had certain reference policies and procedures that would bias its performance, that the data collected were contaminated, or that the instrument had become obtrusive, then that library was dropped and replaced with an alternate. Only responses from libraries that appeared to have been tested in a natural, nonreactive manner were used in the subsequent statistical analysis.

The principle of substitution is widely used, especially in quota sampling. Providing that the substitutes are selected at the same time and by the same method as the rest of the sample, there is no valid reason for their exclusion.[2] Table 2 details the substitutions made in this investigation. Replacements for exposure or instrument failure were made after queries 1, 7, and 14. Additionally, two libraries were replaced for nonresponse to the survey used in this study. The first five libraries in each stratum, which had been originally drawn or replaced, were the forty libraries used in the final analysis. The responses from the remaining thirteen libraries, treated as extras, were discarded prior to final statistical analysis. There was no statistically significant difference between the replaced libraries and their alternates on the major dependent variable, accuracy of response.

Exposed libraries. Difficulties were experienced with data collection to such an extent that exposure eventually took place in eleven libraries, or 16.2 percent of the sixty-eight libraries that were telephoned query 1. In general, the exposed libraries had less than 1,000 FTE students, 50,000

Table 2

NUMBER OF LIBRARIES TESTED, ELIMINATED,
AND ANALYZED BY TYPE OF INSTITUTION AND
CONTROL

| | Two-Yr. | | Four-N. | | Four-G. | | Univ. | | |
	Pub.	Pri.	Pub.	Pri.	Pub.	Pri.	Pub.	Pri.	Totals
Tested query 1	10	12	8	10	7	9	7	5	68
Eliminated									
after query 1	0	2	0	0	0	1	1	0	4
after query 7	1	1	1	2	0	0	0	0	5
after query 14	1	1	1	1	0	0	0	0	4
after survey	0	1	0	0	0	0	1	0	2
as extras	3	2	1	2	2	3	0	0	13
Used in analysis	5	5	5	5	5	5	5	5	40

volumes, 15,000 materials circulated to users, and four FTE professional staff with a graduate degree.

This study demonstrates that it is possible to execute a fourteen round unobtrusive test in small academic libraries. Nevertheless, a potential threat to the unobtrusiveness of the instrument does exist. The instrument became obtrusive first in the smaller institutions, such as Library B, which had only 100 FTE students. The instrument did not become obtrusive in four-year colleges with graduate programs or universities. Libraries in these institutions receive a relatively larger number of telephone reference/information inquiries, and are probably less likely to notice an unobtrusive test.

Survey nonresponse. A survey of academic library

reference/information services was mailed to all fifty-nine libraries that had been telephoned the fourteen queries. The individual responsible for the delivery of reference/information services in three of the libraries did not complete and return the questionnaire. Because the survey response rate was high (94.9 percent) and there was no significant difference on the major dependent variable, it was decided to replace nonresponding libraries with their alternates.

One nonrespondent did not have a stratum alternate, since it was one of only five private universities in the nine southeastern states under study. Thus, only thirty-nine surveys were used in the final analysis. It is interesting to note that this particular library's number of correct responses was the lowest of all universities studied.

Extra libraries. After libraries were eliminated or replaced as necessary, thirteen libraries remained. The data from these libraries, treated as extra, were discarded prior to final statistical analysis. As indicated at the beginning of this chapter (see Table 2), no public or private university libraries were available as extras. As a matter of curiosity, the extra libraries in each stratum were compared on the major dependent variable, with the five libraries in each stratum used in the final statistical analysis. No statistically significant difference was found between the extra and analyzed libraries on the correctness of response or on the three numeric survey sections.

Problems

Data collection difficulties experienced in this investigation occurred for two general reasons: (1) problems encountered with the reference policies and procedures in particular libraries, and (2) problems caused by the nature of the unobtrusive measurement technique itself. Difficulties encountered with the reference policies and procedures in particular libraries centered on limited reference services, staffing patterns, and the legitimacy of the proxy's claim to service. No problems were experienced with cooperative arrangements.

Limited reference services. Some libraries were replaced because they apparently did not offer telephone reference/information services. For example, the telephone conversation with the respondent in Library B revealed that the respondent was a student who thought that it was strange that the inquirer did not come to the library to do her own research. When asked if the reference librarian would be able to help find the information, the student commented: "I don't think we've got one!" Responses from this library and other libraries, telephoned after the investigator considered them exposed, provided evidence that the reference procedure can vary with the status of the inquirer and the length of time that the staff member apparently thought it might take to answer the query.

The pattern of responses from Library I is particularly interesting. Correct answers were received to queries 1 and 2, telephoned respectively on Friday, February 25, in the morning and Wednesday, March 9, in the afternoon. When query 3 was telephoned Thursday afternoon on March 24, 1977, the proxy was immediately asked: "Are you the same person that's been calling with all those in-depth questions? Are you from a book publishing company?" The correct answer was received only after the call was referred to the library director, who indicated that they had been receiving too many phone calls of a similar nature.

The next proxy was questioned as to her name and address. No answer to query 4 was received, and it was suggested that she call her "local library." Correct answers were not received to queries 5 and 6; however, only about one minute was needed to locate the correct answer to the somewhat easier query 7 on May 4.

After two call backs on September 19, the query 8 proxy was referred to "somebody else with more time." A correct answer was given to query 9. While the correct answers were not found for queries 10 and 11, the proxies did not note any unusual questioning.

The query 12 proxy was asked for her name and told: "I don't think you are a student here. You can call back in a little while, if you want to." The proxy did try to call back at several different times; the best response she received was to check with her own library.

When asked for the nearest airport to Warren, Pennsylvania, the query 13 proxy-investigator was told to call the State Department in Pennsylvania or the Chamber of Commerce in Warren. A correct response was not received on query 14. After a three-minute search, the proxy was told:

"We've checked all our reference books and we cannot find that quotation."

In the case of Library I, exposure probably took place on the third query and again on query 12. No particular pattern is discernible regarding a time of day or the day of the week. The reference procedures apparently varied with the query and the status of the user; the lack of a detailed reference policy is evident.

Several other exposed libraries were suspected of having either a policy of reference service with varied levels of assistance or an unexpressed policy of no telephone reference/information service at all! This was evidenced by immediate suggestions to call the public library, unhelpful referrals, and such responses as: "I don't know" or "I have no idea and can't think of any books in the library that would cover it." These responses may also have been a reflection of the staffing pattern of the library's reference department.

Staffing patterns. In two instances, call backs were placed because librarians were not available for unusual reasons. In one case, all librarians were at a funeral; in the other, all librarians were at chapel. While several libraries may have performed as if they were not sufficiently staffed to provide reference/information services during all the hours the test calls were made, only one library specifically mentioned they did not have sufficient personnel to offer telephone reference services. This library also apparently had a policy of varied levels of assistance.

In most instances, it is not known whether the proxy was actually talking to a librarian, a nonprofessional staff member, or a student assistant. However, it was not the intent of this study to test the correctness of response by level of library personnel responding. A service was tested; the responses received would have been received by real students at that institution.

The test took place under normal field conditions during the hours of 9 a.m. to 3:30 p.m. While staffing patterns employed by the various libraries may not have affected the reactivity of the instrument, they did influence the performance of the library. This is as it should be. The librarian who went to lunch leaving the correct answer with the college switchboard operator for the proxy's call back did give better reference service than the librarian who went to lunch and failed to leave a note on the query at the reference desk for her replacement.

Cooperative arrangements. More than one library was sampled in five cities: four libraries in one city, three libraries in another, and two libraries in each of three other cities. Additionally, several libraries apparently were members of institutional systems or consortia with other academic libraries and/or local libraries. One reference network, which included both academic and other types of libraries, was also discovered in the sample. Multiple calls to the same library or even informal sharing among librarians could cause exposure.

Direct calls to other libraries were made for the proxies only on query 4, which was a quotation question. Query 4 was the only query during which a statewide reference network was mentioned. After five call backs and an eight-day delay, one library staff member informed the proxy: "We haven't been able to find it. The State Library was called and they couldn't find it either." Also on query 4, one library staff member called a local public library and a university library (fortunately, not in the sample) for the proxy; two other libraries called faculty members in their English department.

Most frequently, the proxy was told to call other libraries herself as a referral when the correct answer could not be found. While the cooperative arrangements posed a possible threat, no instances of obtrusiveness of the instrument could be traced to this cause.

Proxy's claim to service. Each query had a rationale that permitted a controlled amount of additional information to be supplied by the proxy. The rationale was provided to give the query and the proxy more credibility. It appeared that no query was refused because the library staff member assumed it to be a puzzle, contest, or take-home examination question.

Proxies were instructed to indicate that they were students at the institution, if asked. Nevertheless, the legitimacy of the proxy's claim to service was difficult to maintain.

In both the exposed and nonexposed institutions, the proxy placing a call back frequently did not have to identify herself or the query; it was obviously the only telephone query pending. On the call back to one two-year college, the librarian was reached on her coffee break on the second floor. When the proxy apologized for the interruption, the librarian responded: "That's OK, I told them I was expecting your call." In another library, the proxy was told she could get her question answered when the English classes came to the library for tours the next day.

While only one library actually checked the proxy's name for enrollment status, the proxy's claim to service was compromised in other instances. On the third call back on query 5 to Library D, the proxy was told that research was not done over the telephone and asked the name of her instructor. When the proxy gave the standard response that she did not remember the instructor's name, she was told assistance would be provided if she came to the library and brought her class receipt. In this case and others, it is not clear whether the cause of the exposure was the library's reference policies and procedures or the nature of the unobtrusive measurement technique itself.

Method of inquiry. The method of inquiry itself caused certain difficulties. Using excuses about telephone problems or poor connections, the proxies were able quickly to counter such questions as: "Are you calling long distance?" Library staff members frequently asked the proxy's location before placing the call on hold and searching for the answer; this was probably a courtesy since many of the libraries may have served areas where their students might be calling long distance. In Library C, after the proxy waited fifteen minutes for an answer, the college switchboard operator intercepted the call and stated: "You should call back later since this is a long distance call and I can't locate the librarian who was supposed to be finding the information."

Disconnections occasionally took place due to technical difficulties; in other instances, the library staff member was the cause. For example, in one library the cryptic response was as follows: "Well, I couldn't tell you off the bat. You'll have to call back." Then, the staff member hung up the telephone. The proxy called back twenty minutes later and received a correct answer.

Other difficulties encountered were caused either by the volume of calls or their nature. The proxy's name was requested on occasion by the library staff member because "we need it for these phone requests." In other instances, the proxies were unable to get responses at all. The query 5 proxy in Library G finally gave a false telephone number because, in her words, "the library staff member absolutely insisted on calling me back even though I gave sufficient reason why I couldn't be reached." As previously mentioned, even a book publisher test was suspected.

It is important to emphasize that the performance of academic libraries in this study was successfully measured on fact-type queries asked via telephone. The difficulties experienced have been recounted for future researchers; however, since all exposed libraries were replaced, the data subjected to final analysis were not contaminated.

Queries

The fourteen queries that constituted the performance test in this study are displayed in Table 3 along with the percentage of correct responses. Each query will be discussed individually, followed by observations on the queries as a group. The numbers and letters in parentheses following the book titles throughout this section are references to the full bibliographic information in Sheehy.[3]

Query 1: Who was Secretary of State when Sumner Welles was his assistant?

Answer: Cordell Hull.

As indicated in Table 3, thirty-nine correct responses, or 97.5 percent of all responses, were received to query 1, which was telephoned from February 21 through February 25, 1977.

Thirteen individuals who gave the correct response did not require a call back. The fastest correct answer was received in one minute and fifty-five seconds.

Nine respondents, or 22.5 percent, volunteered the sources they consulted. Who's Who in America (AJ57) was

Table 3

PERCENTAGE OF CORRECT RESPONSES BY QUERY

Percent correct (N = 40)		Query
97.5	1.	Who was Secretary of State when Sumner Welles was his assistant?
30.0	2.	What is the symbol for a population mean?
90.0	3.	What are the names of the books that make up Lawrence Durrell's Alexandrian tetralogy?
25.0	4.	Who said something like: the naïve and the beautiful have no enemy but time?
2.5	5.	When was George Washington given the title of General of the Armies of the United States?
7.5	6.	Who is the president of the American Society for Information Science?
40.0	7.	What is the Zip Code for Behrend College in Erie, Pennsylvania?
87.5	8.	When did China orbit its first satellite?
65.0	9.	Is the book Albert Einstein and the Cosmic World Order, by Cornelius Lanczos, recommended for laymen?
10.0	10.	What is the address of Mexico City College?
72.5	11.	Who is the President of the American Library Association?
85.0	12.	Who were the stars in the 1960 Broadway Production of Camelot?
55.0	13.	Where is the nearest airport to Warren, Pennsylvania?
37.5	14.	Who said: "There are two good things in life, freedom of thought and freedom of action"?

the title most frequently cited by those who found the acceptable answer; the second was <u>World Almanac</u> (CG75).

Although one-step sources exist, most respondents evidently followed a two-step process, as indicated by the titles cited. First, they read a biographical account to find when Welles assisted the Secretary of State. Then, they consulted another source, such as an almanac, to locate the name of the Secretary of State. The public university library staff member who did not find the correct answer was also following a two-step process. After a three and one-half minute search, she stated that she was unable to respond because "apparently Sumner Welles was never an Assistant Secretary of State."

Query 2: What is the symbol for a population mean?

Answer: μ or mu.

Thirty percent, or twelve out of forty libraries, found the acceptable answer to query 2. Eight referrals were received from respondents who did not find the correct answer; most of these recognized the statistical nature of the question. Some library staff members assumed population was synonymous with inhabitants. In one library, the respondent observed:

> We only found the symbol for population, which is a circle with four dots inside. Come in and check the book on zero population growth by Paul Ehrlich; it should give you the symbol for the population mean.

Two of the library staff members who gave the correct answer did not require a call back. One of these respondents answered in four minutes; the other answered instantaneously.

Only one library staff member with the correct answer volunteered the title used: <u>Dictionary/Outline of Basic Statistics</u> (CG26). The correct answer can also be easily located in almost any basic statistics textbook and the <u>McGraw-Hill Encyclopedia of Science and Technology</u> (EA 107).

Query 3: What are the names of the books that make up Lawrence Durrell's Alexandrian tetralogy?

Answer: Justine, Balthazar, Mountolive, and Clea.

Thirty-six library staff members, or 90 percent of all libraries called, correctly located the series of books that comprise Lawrence Durrell's Alexandria Quartet. Twenty-five of the respondents with the correct answer did not require a call back. The fastest correct response was received in thirty seconds; the median length of time was about three minutes. Despite the speed with which libraries located the correct answer, two library staff members suggested that the proxy come to the library in person because "it would take too long to look them up."

Eight (20 percent) of the library staff members actually volunteered the source of their answer. Because the investigator was interested in how many library staff members actually answered the query from holdings information, the proxy was instructed to request the source, if it was not volunteered.

The title most frequently used to locate the correct answer was Books in Print (AA473), with ten citations. The library's card catalog was cited by seven respondents; one staff member mentioned both the card catalog and Books in Print. Contemporary Authors (AJ33) was cited by five staff members. Three respondents used the Alexandria Quartet itself to answer query 3.[4] Other respondents cited standard literature handbooks, encyclopedias, or biographical sources.

Query 4: Who said something like: the naïve and the beautiful have no enemy but time?

Answer: William Butler Yeats, who wrote: "The innocent and the beautiful have no enemy but time."

The answer can be located in the 14th edition of Bartlett's _Familiar Quotations_ (BD98) using access points under the words "enemy" or "time." Although the quotation was exact except for one word, only ten libraries (25 percent) found the correct answer. Two library staff members who found the acceptable answer did not require a call back. The fastest correct answer was received in about two minutes.

Twelve of the forty respondents (30 percent) volunteered the sources they used. Five of the ten library staff members who found the correct answer indicated that they had used _Familiar Quotations_; seven of the thirty library staff members who did not find the correct answer also cited this source.

As indicated previously in the chapter, library staff called faculty in English departments and other libraries for the proxy on this query. Thirteen referrals were received from the thirty library staff members who did not find the acceptable answer; two of these offered substitute quotations.

Since the investigator knew that the correct response to this query was dependent upon access to the 14th (1968) edition of _Familiar Quotations_, the libraries were telephoned again in January 1978 regarding ownership of this source. Thirty of the respondents, or 75 percent, indicated that their library owned the 14th edition of Bartlett. This ownership percentage is somewhat low considering that all libraries in this sample were established before the 14th edition was published; this standard reference book is still listed in _Books in Print_.

It cannot be certain that the responses received to the holdings question in January were correct or that they were an accurate reflection of ownership of the title in April 1977; however, the data do tend to indicate that library staff members chose the path of least resistance in answering query 4. No library that did not own the 14th edition of Bartlett's correctly answered query 4. Only 33.3 percent (ten of the thirty libraries that owned the source) found the acceptable answer. Many staff members probably checked the index only under "naive" or "beautiful," where no access points were found.

Query 5: When was George Washington given the title of General of the Armies of the United States?

Answer: 1976.

Only one respondent located the acceptable answer for this query. The library staff member, who stated that he had remembered reading about it recently, located the correct answer in six minutes and forty-seven seconds using the Congressional Index Service (CK89). Public Law 94-479 could also have been located in other reference books that cover Congressional activity or in the New York Times Index (AF67); however, the staff member would first have had to be aware of the current nature of the query.

In contrast to the performance on other queries, 80 percent of the respondents cited the source of their answer on query 5. Of the thirty-two library staff members who mentioned the source of their incorrect answer, twenty-two (69 percent) used an encyclopedia or an almanac. If the query were telephoned today, performance would improve; the correct answer has since appeared in the new edition of World Almanac (CG75) and in other sources.

Query 6: Who is the president of the American Society for Information Science?

Answer: Margaret Fischer.

One of the respondents found the correct answer in two and one-half minutes. Only three library staff members, or 7.5 percent, located the acceptable answer; none cited their source.

Of the thirty-seven respondents who did not give the correct answer, five cited a source. Most of these and other respondents with the incorrect answer used the Encyclopedia of Associations (CA67), which listed Joshua I. Smith, the former executive director.

Two library staff members gave the name of Melvin Day, the immediate past-president of ASIS at the time this query was telephoned in late April and the first week of May 1977. Due to a publication lag, current issues of both the Journal and the Bulletin still indicated that Melvin Day was president. To locate the acceptable answer, library staff members would have also had to check when the officers changed. The acceptable answer could have been found in the ALA Yearbook. [5]

Query 7: What is the Zip Code for Behrend College in Erie, Pennsylvania?

Answer: 16510.

Sixteen respondents, or 40 percent, located the correct answer to query 7; fourteen of these answered without a call back. The fastest correct answer was received in thirty seconds; the median time required for the correct answer was about one and one-half minutes.

The acceptable answer to query 7 was not easily located in standard directories of colleges and universities because Behrend College, usually listed under Pennsylvania State University, is not always cross-referenced. There was an index access point under Behrend in the 1976 edition of Lovejoy's College Guide (CB151).

Six respondents, or 15 percent of all libraries called, cited the specific source used to locate their answer. The title most frequently mentioned by the respondents with the correct answer was the National ZIP Code Directory (CH300), which was also mentioned by respondents who failed to find the correct answer.

Several library staff members gave incorrect Zip Codes, such as 16500, which is the code for Erie as a whole and not Behrend. Only eight of the twenty-four respondents who failed to find the correct answer made referrals; four to the post office, one to the telephone company's "information," and three to public libraries.

Query 8: When did China orbit its first satellite?

Answer: 1970.

Thirty of the thirty-five library staff members who found the acceptable answer required at least one call back. The fastest correct answer was found in fifty-two seconds.

Fourteen respondents mentioned a source. The titles most frequently cited by the staff members who located the correct answer were World Almanac (CG75), Encyclopaedia Britannica (AC2), and the New York Times Index (AF67). One enterprising library staff member, who had evidently used Readers' Guide to Periodical Literature (AE169), cited the correct answer from a U.S. News and World Report article in 1970.

Query 9: Is the book Albert Einstein and the Cosmic World Order, by Cornelius Lanczos, recommended for laymen?

Answer: Yes.

The simple acceptable answer for this query was "yes"; however, most of the twenty-six respondents who gave the correct answer also explained why the book was recommended for laymen or cited their source. The fastest correct answer was received in sixty-one seconds. Twenty library staff members who gave the correct answer required a call back.

The most frequently used title was Book Review Digest (AA411). Other sources used to find the answer included Choice (AA353), Reader's Advisor (AA339), and personal knowledge/personal examination of the books. Two library staff members referred the proxy to physics professors, who gave acceptable answers.

The sources most often used by the library staff who failed to locate the acceptable answer were personal knowledge

or the library's card catalog. One respondent actually used
Book Review Digest but did not locate the correct answer.

Query 10: What is the address of Mexico City College?

Answer: Puebla, Mexico.

Staff members in only four libraries, or 10 percent
of all libraries called, located the acceptable answer; all required call backs.

Eleven respondents (27.5 percent) mentioned the references they consulted. Three of the four library staff members who found the acceptable answer cited their sources as
follows: a librarian who went to school in Mexico and Study
Abroad (CB200); a woman in the library from Mexico and a
reference book; World of Learning (CB132) because the answer "wasn't in Study Abroad."

The rationale for query 10 was as follows: Someone
in one of my classes told me that it is a very good school
and has recently become a university. This rationale, given
with each application of the query, provided a clue for locating the correct answer. Mexico City College, founded in
1940, has been known as the University of the Americas or
Universidad de las Americas since 1963. The acceptable answer could have been found in current editions of World of
Learning and Study Abroad; however, it is not indexed under
Mexico City College. The library staff member would have
had to browse through the entries under Mexico in World of
Learning or use another lead-in tool, such as a librarian
from Mexico, to find the institution's name change and then
the current address. At the time query 10 was telephoned,
The International Handbook was not sufficiently up-to-date to
provide the Puebla address.

In January 1978, the libraries were telephoned the following holdings question; Do you have a recent edition of
World of Learning? Twenty-six library staff members (65
percent) indicated that their library owned a 1972 or later
edition of World of Learning that could have been used to

locate the acceptable answer to query 10. While it is not known if the responses to the question in January 1978 were an accurate reflection of the library's holdings in October 1977, the data tend to indicate that only 15.4 percent, or four out of twenty-six, of the library staff members who probably could have found the acceptable answer actually did so.

Ten of the respondents who failed to find the acceptable answer to query 10 offered referrals. Eight offered the address of another college in Mexico. One suggested that the proxy come to the library. Another respondent suggested that the proxy call the Admissions Office; a correct answer was not received.

Query 11: Who is the president of the American Library Association?

Answer: Eric Moon.

Twenty-nine (72.5 percent) of the respondents found the acceptable answer; fifteen of these did not require a call back. The median length of time required for the correct answer was a little over one minute. One correct and one incorrect answer were received instantaneously.

Six of the library staff members, or 15 percent of all respondents, volunteered the source of their answers. The sources mentioned included Bowker Annual (AB118), the ALA Yearbook, and the Encyclopedia of Associations (CA67). Respondents who gave the incorrect answer also mentioned these titles.

Five of the eleven library staff members who failed to find the acceptable answer gave the name of Clara Jones, who was the immediate past-president at the time this query telephoned from October 24 through November 1, 1977. Inaccurate answers cannot always be explained by the use of outdated sources. At least two of the respondents, who gave an incorrect answer, were too up-to-date; they gave the name of Russell Shank, the ALA president-elect at that time. Two respondents were unable to locate the name of the president but suggested that the proxy write Robert Wedgeworth, who was the executive director. Two other respondents insisted that Robert Wedgeworth was the ALA president!

Query 12: Who were the stars in the 1960 Broadway Production of Camelot?

Answer: Richard Burton, Robert Goulet, Julie Andrews.

The rationale for query 12 requested the names of the stars who played Arthur, Lancelot, and Guinevere; the acceptable answers respectively were Richard Burton, Robert Goulet, and Julie Andrews. One library staff member found two of the three stars; her answer was not treated as correct. Respondents in thirty-four libraries (85 percent) found the acceptable answer.

The fastest correct answer was actually received instantaneously; however, the proxy was instructed to call back so that the answer could be verified. Most respondents who answered without a call back required about three minutes to locate the correct answer.

Seven of the respondents who found the acceptable answer cited their source. The most frequently mentioned titles were the New York Times Index (AF67) or the New York Times Theatre Reviews (BG24). Other staff members who found the correct answer used specialized handbooks on New York theater, texts on musical comedy, or reviews in periodicals (e.g., Time).

Query 12 was specifically constructed by the investigator to parallel a question used in a previous obtrusive study. 6 In 1967, Goldhor found that eight out of twelve libraries (66.7 percent) located the correct answer to the following question: "Who were the stars in the 1960 production of 'Under the Yum Yum Tree'?" The academic library staff members in this study had a larger percentage of correct answers than the public library staff members in the Goldhor study.

Query 13: Where is the nearest airport to Warren, Pennsylvania?

Answer: Jamestown, New York.

Twenty-two library staff members, or 55 percent of all libraries called, gave correct responses to query 13, which was telephoned just prior to Thanksgiving. Four did not require a call back.

A little over three minutes was needed for the fastest correct answer received without a call back. One private four-year college without graduate programs actually had a faster answer. After about a two-minute search, the library staff member suggested:

> We don't have anything in the library to help you. Call the Academic Dean's office; he does a lot of traveling and might be able to help you.

The Secretary to the Academic Dean found the acceptable answer in just forty-two seconds.

Specific titles were seldom cited by the library staff members; however, most mentioned consulting atlases, gazetteers, flight maps, airline guides, and/or guidebooks. Two respondents with the correct answer cited the Rand McNally Commercial Atlas (CL218a); another cited Editor and Publisher's Market Guide (CH495). The acceptable answer can also be easily located in such sources as the National Geographic Atlas of the World (CL211) and the World Aviation Directory (EH70).

Query 13 had more referrals than any other query because seven respondents who gave the correct answer also suggested the proxy check with a travel agent, an airline, or an airport. One respondent who gave the correct answer also supplied the toll-free (800) telephone number of a major airline.

Query 13 was constructed by the investigator to parallel a question used in a previous unobtrusive study by Childers, who found that questions in his category "geographical facts" prompted fewer correct answers than would be expected under the laws of probability.[7] In the Childers study, the question in the "geographical facts" category with the lowest number of correct answers, and the lowest of all twenty-six questions telephoned, was question 11. Only four correct answers (16 percent) were received on question 11, which was called as follows: "Where is the nearest commercial airport to Rio Grande, Ohio?" Childers did not list the acceptable answers for this question; apparently, the answer to his question 11, then and now, is Huntington, West Virginia.

Query 13 in this study also had an airport in another state as the acceptable answer. The academic library staff members, with 55 percent of the answers correct, appear to have performed better than the public library staff members, who had only 16 percent of the answers correct.

Query 14: Who said: "There are two good things in life, freedom of thought and freedom of action"?

Answer: William Somerset Maugham.

Fifteen of the forty respondents (37.5 percent) found the acceptable answer to this query. Only two library staff members who gave correct answers did not require call backs; the fastest of these was two minutes and forty-five seconds. Thirty-six respondents, more than on any other query, required at least one call back.

Six of the twenty-five staff members who failed to find the correct answer made referrals. Two suggested that the proxy call another library in the area; four staff members offered substitute quotations.

The acceptable answer to query 14 can be found using several access points in either the 12th or 13th edition of Bartlett's Familiar Quotations (BD98); the answer is not in the 14th (1968) edition. The importance of the previous editions of Familiar Quotations has been noted as follows:

> In recent editions many quotations previously included have been omitted, and many new ones added.

Earlier editions, particularly the 12th, should not be discarded, as they will include quotations not found in the latest edition.[8]

At the conclusion of the performance test, the libraries were telephoned to inquire about their ownership of various sources. Thirty-one library staff members (77.5 percent) indicated that their library owned either the 12th or the 13th edition of Bartlett's Familiar Quotations. No library that did not own the source correctly answered query 14; however, sixteen respondents who apparently had the source in their collection failed to find the answer. Only 48.4 percent of the respondents who probably had the source in their collection in December 1977 correctly answered query 14.

Query 14 was constructed by the investigator to parallel a question used in a previous unobtrusive study. In the appendix of his study, Crowley mentions that only one library out of twelve (8 percent) found the correct answer to the following question:

Who is the author of this quotation: "The storm arrived and was no surprise to the barometer."[9]

The answer, Norman Curwin, was in the 12th (1948) edition of Bartlett's Familiar Quotations but had been dropped from the 13th (1955) edition. The academic library staff members in this study, with 37.5 percent of the answers correct, performed better than the public library staff members, who had only 8 percent of the answers correct on a similar query.

Performance

Table 4 summarizes the performance on the fourteen queries for the forty librarians. Only 282 of the 560 responses, or 50.4 percent, were acceptable answers. At least one call back was required in 380 instances, or 55 percent of all observations. The median number of call backs was slightly more than one. The maximum was four call backs (queries 4 and 13).

Considering only the correct responses, 65.9 percent (183) were made after at least one call back. The median length of time for a correct answer, without a call back, was approximately three minutes. In libraries that were eventually credited with a correct response, the median search time before suggesting a call back was approximately four minutes.

Table 4

PERFORMANCE DISTRIBUTION FOR THE
MINOR DEPENDENT VARIABLES ON FOURTEEN
QUERIES BY ACCURACY OF RESPONSE

Minor Dependent Variables	All Responses (N=560)	Correct Responses (N=282)	Incorrect Responses (N=278)
Refusal received	32	0	32
Referral made	87	9	78
Call back required			
#	308	183	125
Median	1	1	1
Minimum	1	1	1
Maximum	4	3	4
Answered immediately			
#	252	99	153
Median (in seconds)	154	183	150
Minimum (in seconds)	01	01	01
Maximum (in seconds)	900	620	900
Attempted then call back			
#	71	35	36
Median (in seconds)	220	232	190
Minimum (in seconds)	01	01	01
Maximum (in seconds)	1040	1040	900
Source volunteered	150	70	80

Staff members cited the source of their response in 150 instances, or 26.8 percent. The most frequently mentioned source was Bartlett's Familiar Quotations. Seventeen citations of this title are not surprising, since it was the only known source for the acceptable answer to two queries. Thirteen respondents mentioned using the library's card catalog, which was the second most frequently mentioned source.

As indicated in Table 4, library staff members who did

not find the acceptable answer were more likely to make referrals, not require a call back, take less time in searching for an answer, and volunteer the source used than were the library staff members who did find the acceptable answer. It should be pointed out that thirty-two refusals to answer were received from library staff members who did not find the acceptable answer; these refusals constituted 5.7 percent of all observations and 11.5 percent of all incorrect responses. The library staff members who did not find the acceptable answer performed efficiently, as they required fewer call backs and searched for only about two and one-half minutes before responding; however, they were hardly more effective respondents, failing to perform on the major dependent variable, accuracy of response.

Only 27.6 percent of the 282 respondents who failed to find the acceptable answer made referrals. The most frequent referrals (50.3 percent) were either substitute answers or suggestions to come to the library, call other offices on campus, or check other types of materials in that library or another library. Twenty-four referrals were specifically made to other libraries; public libraries were the most popular. There were eighteen referrals to public libraries, or 75 percent of all referrals to other libraries. Fourteen referrals, or 17.9 percent of all referrals, were made to external agencies, such as the post office or a travel agency.

If a call back was required before receiving a response, proxies were allowed to make arrangements to place the call back at a time convenient to themselves and the library staff members. If the library staff member did not specify a time for the call back, the proxy was instructed to suggest a half-hour interval. The time delay between the initial call and the first call back was not included in Table 4 because it was not subject to control by the investigator; however, the first call back was placed in less than two hours about 70 percent of the time. Only a relatively small number of calls (10.4 percent) required more than one working day before the first call back.

At the beginning of this investigation, it was arbitrarily decided to weight the search time on each call back by fifteen minutes. Only nine of the 307 initial call backs were actually placed in fifteen minutes or less. Nevertheless, fifteen minutes appears to be a reasonable choice of search time. As indicated by the data in Table 4, the maximum search time was fifteen minutes on the responses given im-

mediately without suggesting a call back. The maximum
search time was seventeen minutes and twenty seconds on
the responses attempted immediately before suggesting a call
back.

The reasons for the failure to provide a correct answer are related to factors other than the search time. The
proxies allowed the library staff as much time as they needed
to search for the correct answer; each query received at
least one correct answer; all queries, except query 10, were
rapidly answered without a call back at least once. The chief
cause of failure seems to center on the source of the response. There is evidence that in some cases the library
may not have owned the proper source and staff did not use
other resources. At other times, the library apparently
owned the proper source, but staff either did not use it or
used it improperly.

Since Bartlett's Familiar Quotations was a standard
reference title, the investigator never suspected that 25 percent of the libraries would not own the in-print 14th edition.
However, since a service and not holdings were being tested,
these libraries were not given performance credit for not
owning the source. Some library staff used very imaginative
approaches to go beyond their holdings or to develop additional source access points. Library staff who asked a woman from Mexico, called an English professor, suggested the
Academic Dean's office, or were able to interpret correctly
the information in the National ZIP Code Directory deserve
higher performance scores.

There is some evidence that the currentness of the
query did make finding the correct answer more difficult,
as discussed under queries 5 and 6. Familiarity with the
subject of the query did help improve performance in some
cases, as indicated by the responses to query 11.

There are some additional indications that performance
on a particular query is more influenced by the sources
needed and the staff's ability to exploit the sources than by
the subject classification of the query. Library staff members performed poorest on queries that could not easily be
answered with the usual answer-providing tools.

As indicated previously in this chapter, even if the library owned an appropriate source, there was no guarantee
that the library staff member would be willing or able to use
that source.

The Performance Test and Sample Size

The adequacy of any test depends to a certain extent on the care with which the test items have been selected, the difficulty and discrimination of the items, and the reliability and validity of the test results. The queries chosen for this study were either actual fact-type queries or close simulations of real queries.

It was felt that the fourteen queries selected had content validity. That is, the items would measure performance differences, if any, among academic libraries on fact-type queries asked by telephone. Additionally, the test had objectivity in that the acceptable answers to each query were predetermined short answers that could be consistently scored either correct or not correct.

Indices of item difficulty and item discrimination were computed for each query. Based on these calculations, query 1, which had only one incorrect answer, and query 5, which had only one correct answer, did not appear to be worthwhile items. Since the performance on these queries may have been more accidental than a true reflection of the performance of the two libraries involved, the queries were dropped from further analysis. As will be shown in the next chapter, the elimination of queries 1 and 5 had no significant effect on the findings on the major dependent variable for the classifications of academic libraries.

A Spearman rank order correlation between randomly assigned test halves was computed and the Spearman-Brown Prophecy Formula used to estimate the reliability of the twelve query performance test, which was .58. A coefficient of .50 or .60 is usually considered sufficient to differentiate between groups.

Thus, a reliability coefficient of .58 provides the consistency that would make validity possible. Furthermore, as previously mentioned, the items that comprise the performance test were carefully selected to ensure content validity. The results of this study (50.4 percent correct) are consistent with the results of previous unobtrusive studies, which provides further evidence for the validity of the results of the performance test in this study.

Adequacy of sample size. The formula and tables in King and Bryant were used to check the adequacy of the sample size.[10] The overall sample was considered adequate for an exploratory study. The 480 observations had a standard error of 2.27 percent. The 95-percent confidence interval for the true percentage of correct answers was between 45.96 and 54.87 percent.

With certain formula adjustments, the disproportionate stratified sample drawn for this study can be related to the 361 academic libraries in the nine southeastern states that comprise the population. Selection and weighting is done separately and independently for each stratum and then summed across all strata.[11] Weights were applied to the major dependent variable to represent the proportion of the population elements in the stratum (see Table 1) so that the sum of the weights across all strata equaled one, in essence a 100-percent "sample."

The responses, weighted for the proportion of the population actually sampled, had a mean of 49.12 percent on the major dependent variable, accuracy of response, and a standard error of .76 percent on the twelve-query unobtrusive test. One can be 95 percent confident that the 361 academic libraries in the Southeast would have found the acceptable answers 49 percent of the time ($\pm$ 1.5%).

4.
FINDINGS: LIBRARY CLASSIFICATIONS

The findings presented in this chapter relate to the second major research question of this study:

Are there differences in effectiveness among academic libraries classified as to type of control and/or type of institution?

The performance by the type of institution and control is displayed in Appendix D, which details the major dependent variable, accuracy of response, along with the minor dependent variables for the twelve queries subjected to final analysis. The first step in answering the research question was to accumulate the observations recorded during the performance test for eight dependent variables to create performance scores for each library.

The performance score for the major dependent variable equaled the number of correct responses on the twelve queries. Statistics describing the number of correct answers by library classification are presented in Appendix E. Performance scores for the minor dependent variables were arrived at by summing the occurrence (yes = 1) on the twelve queries for the following variables: response refusal, call back, referral, response made immediately, response attempted then call back suggested, and source of response volunteered.

An additional minor dependent variable referred to as total time was created by adding the length of time (in seconds) on the responses attempted immediately, the length of time (in seconds) on the responses attempted immediately be-

[61]

fore suggesting a call back, and the total number of call backs required multiplied by fifteen minutes (900 seconds). As indicated in the last chapter, the decision to weight the number of call backs by fifteen minutes appears reasonable since the maximum search time on responses received without a call back was exactly fifteen minutes.

Selected minor dependent variables were also controlled for effectiveness by isolating the correct responses and summing the minor dependent variables. The following variables were not controlled by the accuracy of the responses: refusals, with nine occurrences if the response was correct, and referrals, with no occurrences if the response was correct.

The thirteen dependent variables analyzed are separately discussed for the three classifications of academic libraries, which are as follows: (1) type of control--public or private; (2) type of institution--two-year colleges, four-year colleges with or without graduate programs, or universities; and (3) type of institution and control, e.g., public or private two-year colleges. When differences on the major dependent variables were significant at the .05 level or less, comparisons were made with the peripheral independent variables that might have influenced the result, such as the time of day of the initial telephone call. The last section in this chapter notes findings on the major dependent variable when all fourteen queries are analyzed.

Type of Control

The Mann-Whitney U test was used to examine the performance scores on each of the thirteen dependent variables and the differences, if any, between twenty privately controlled and twenty publicly controlled academic libraries. There was no significant difference in central tendency between public and private academic libraries on the number of correct answers and eleven of the twelve minor dependent variables. On the minor variable "answered immediately," there was a significant difference when the responses were controlled by accuracy of the response. The public academic library staff members were significantly more likely to answer correctly immediately.

Public academic library staff members were not necessarily more efficient and effective than staff in private academic libraries just because they answered more queries correctly immediately. While private academic library staff members were more likely to require at least one call back, they also found more correct answers (123) than the public academic library staff members (119). Furthermore, there was no significant difference in the total time for all responses or for correct responses between public and private academic libraries. For these reasons, it appears more appropriate to conclude that there was no real difference in effectiveness when the libraries were classified as to type of control.

Type of Institution

The Kruskal-Wallis one-way analysis of variance by ranks was used to examine the thirteen dependent variables and the differences, if any, between the forty academic libraries classified by type of institution. The Kruskal-Wallis H, which is somewhat similar to the parametric F statistic, tests differences in central tendency among more than two groups using the rank value of each case.

The results of the Kruskal-Wallis one-way analysis of variance are summarized in Table 5. There was a significant difference for the major dependent variable and for two of the twelve minor dependent variables at the .05 level. Universities and four-year colleges with graduate programs had higher medians than two-year colleges and four-year colleges without graduate programs on the three of the dependent variables that were significantly different. Each of the major and minor dependent variables that were significantly different by type of institution will be discussed in turn below.

Performance score: response

Summary statistics that further describe the number of correct answers by type of institution are presented in Table B of Appendix E. While there was slightly more dispersion in the number of correct responses in the universities, there was a regular and progressive increase in effectiveness from two-year colleges to universities as measured by either the median or the mean. This pattern is also evident in the medians displayed in Table 5.

Individual comparisons were made using the Mann-Whitney U to test which groups were significantly different. Table 6 details the probabilities resulting from the six Mann-Whitney U tests for the number of correct responses by type

Table 5

MEDIAN PERFORMANCE SCORES BY TYPE OF INSTITUTION

Performance Score	Libraries			
	Two-Yr. (N=10)	Four-N. (N=10)	Four-G. (N=10)	Univ.
Response Correct, no.	5.0*	5.5*	6.5*	7.5*
Refusal received All responses, no.	1.5	.9	.2	.2
Referral made All responses, no.	2.2	2.5	2.5	1.1
Call back required All responses, no.	6.5	6.7	6.9	6.2
Correct responses, no.	3.5	3.7	4.7	3.5
Answered immediately All responses, no.	5.5	5.2	5.1	5.8
Correct responses, no.	1.0	1.7	2.0	3.2
Attempted then call back All responses, no.	.8	1.8	2.0	1.8
Correct responses, no.	.3	.3	.9	1.0
Time (in hours) All responses	2.4	2.2	2.5	2.1
Correct responses	1.1	1.2	1.4	1.0
Source volunteered All responses, no.	1.2*	2.0*	3.5*	3.0*
Correct responses, no.	.5*	.3*	2.2*	2.2*

*p < .05 Kruskal-Wallis one-way analysis of variance by ranks corrected for ties.

of institution. The performance score on the major dependent variable for the two-year colleges was different from four-year colleges with graduate programs and universities at the .05 level of significance. The effectiveness of four-year colleges without graduate programs was significantly different from that of universities at the .05 level. Also indicated in Table 6 is the fact that most of the groups differed in effectiveness at the .10 level of significance.

Table 6

MATRIX OF PROBABILITIES* ON NUMBER OF CORRECT RESPONSES BY TYPE OF INSTITUTION

	Two-Yr. (N=10)	Four-N. (N=10)	Four-G. (N=10)	Univ. (N=10)
Two-Yr.	. . .			
Four-N.	n. s. *	. . .		
Four-G.	.010	.067	. . .	
Univ.	.006	.018	.079	. . .

*Probabilities from six separate Mann-Whitney U tests corrected for ties; n. s. means $\underline{p}$ > .10.

Performance score: source volunteered

There was a significant difference by type of institution for the number of times a source was volunteered on all responses and on correct responses. Subsequent Mann-Whitney U tests indicated that there was a significant difference at the .05 level between two-year colleges and four-year colleges with graduate programs on the number of times at least one source was volunteered for all responses. There was also a significant difference between four-year colleges without graduate programs and four-year colleges with graduate programs on the number of times at least one source was volunteered on all responses.

When the number of times at least one source was volunteered was controlled for effectiveness, four-year colleges without graduate programs differed significantly from four-year colleges with graduate programs and from universities. Two-year colleges differed significantly from four-year colleges with graduate programs and almost differed at the .05 level from universities as to the mean rank number of times at least one source was volunteered on correct responses. There was no difference at the .10 level or less between two-year colleges and four-year colleges without graduate programs or between four-year colleges with graduate programs and universities on the number of times at least one source was volunteered on either correct responses or all responses.

The pattern on sources volunteered parallels the pattern of correct responses on the major dependent variable. While there does appear to be evidence that the more effective academic libraries are also more likely to volunteer the source of their response, it should be pointed out that sources were volunteered on only 108, or 22.5 percent, of the 480 responses.

The percentage distribution of sources volunteered by the major dependent variable, displayed in Table 7, provides a clearer indication of the relationship between sources volunteered, correctness of response, and the type of institution. While library staff members in four-year colleges with graduate programs and universities were more likely to volunteer the source of their response, they were apparently more likely to do so if the answer was correct. In contrast, staff in four-year colleges without graduate programs were more likely to volunteer the source of their response if the answer was not correct. Two-year college library staff members were just as likely to volunteer the source of the response for correct answers or for answers which were not correct.

Only a small percentage of the respondents volunteered the source used. The number of times at least one source was volunteered ranged from 15 percent in the two-year colleges to 30 percent in the four-year colleges with graduate programs. While the findings indicate there is apparently some relationship between the volunteering of the source used and the accuracy of the response, staff members in all types of institutions infrequently volunteered the source of their response.

Table 7

PERCENTAGE DISTRIBUTION OF PERFORMANCE ON THE MINOR DEPENDENT VARIABLE: SOURCE VOLUNTEERED BY ACCURACY OF RESPONSE AND TYPE OF INSTITUTION

Source Volunteered by Response	Libraries				Totals
	Two-Yr.	Four-N.	Four-G.	Univ.	
Source volunteered					
Response correct	7.5%	5.0%	18.3%	19.2%	12.5%
Response not correct	7.5	11.7	11.7	9.2	10.0
Source not volunteered					
Response correct	35.0	40.0	35.8	40.8	37.9
Response not correct	50.0	43.3	34.1	30.8	39.6
Totals	100.0% (N=120)	100.0% (N=120)	100.0% (N=120)	100.0% (N=120)	100.0% (N=480)

Type of Institution and Control

Each of the four types of institutions was separately examined using the Mann-Whitney U to test for differences, if any, in the dependent variables between the five privately controlled and five publicly controlled academic libraries for that type of institution. The statistical null hypothesis was rejected in favor of the alternate hypothesis for the major dependent variable only for the four-year colleges without graduate programs (four-N). Both public and private four-year colleges without graduate programs had similar dispersion pattern on the number of correct answers; however, private libraries (median 6.2) were significantly more effective than public (median 4.2) as measured by the Mann-Whitney U test and as indicated by the measure of central tendency displayed in Table C of Appendix E.

When the minor dependent variables were controlled for correctness of the response, the staff members in private four-year colleges without graduate programs (median 4.3) were significantly more likely to require a call back than the staff members in the public four-year colleges without graduate programs (median 2.7). While there was no difference, at the .10 level or less, between public and private four-year colleges without graduate programs on the number of times a response was attempted immediately or the number of times a response was attempted immediately and then a call back suggested, there was a significant difference in the number of times a response was attempted immediately and then a call back suggested when this minor variable was controlled for the correctness of the response. The staff members in public four-year colleges without graduate programs have the dubious distinction of finding none of the acceptable answers in the five instances they attempted a response before suggesting a call back. This was the only case of zero success for any of the library classifications.

While there was no difference in the total time required between the libraries, if the response was correct, the staff members in private four-year colleges without graduate programs (median 1.5) required significantly more time than the staff members in public four-year colleges without graduate programs (median .8). The staff in private four-year colleges without graduate programs required twenty-four call backs for their thirty-two correct responses. While the staff in public four-year colleges without graduate programs found only twenty-two correct answers, they required only twelve call backs; exactly half the number of call backs required by their colleagues in private libraries when the response was correct.

The findings indicate that there was a difference in effectiveness between public and private four-year colleges without graduate programs. Staff in private four-year colleges without graduate programs found a significantly larger number of correct answers. While they were more effective, the staff in the four-year private colleges without graduate programs were less efficient from a patron's viewpoint in that they required more call backs and time delays on these correct answers.

There were no differences in effectiveness when the university libraries and the four-year colleges with graduate programs were classified as to type of control.

Other Variables

There were significant differences in the number of correct answers when the academic libraries were classified by type of institution, as well as between public and private four-year colleges without graduate programs. The original observations, which constituted the performance test, were examined to see if the significant differences might be due to other variables which the investigator did not or could not control.

Peripheral independent variables

Because of the potential threat of exposure through cooperative arrangements, the investigator monitored the libraries' consortia membership, city, state, and telephone area code. In addition to making the initial telephone contacts at a randomly assigned time and day of the week, the proxies recorded the sex of the responding library staff member throughout the performance test. The results of the series of chi-square tests involving performance on the major dependent variable, accuracy of response, and these other independent variables indicated that the findings on the major dependent variable did not appear to be influenced by the peripheral variables.

Queries 1 and 5

As discussed in Chapter 3, queries 1 and 5 were dropped from further analysis because they had little discriminative power. While the elimination of these two queries did not change the proportion of acceptable answers in the sample, it did change the performance scores on the major dependent variable in two libraries. One public four-year college with graduate programs, which gave the only acceptable answer to query 5, had its performance score reduced by one. One public university, which gave the only incorrect answer to query 1, had its performance score on the major dependent variable increased by one.

The findings on effectiveness among academic libraries classified as to type of control and/or type of institution were checked to ascertain if the elimination of queries 1 and 5 had affected the results. None of the findings on the major dependent variable were changed by the elimination of queries 1 and 5. The Kruskal-Wallis H test for difference by type of institution on all fourteen queries was 12.8, which was significant at .005.

5.
FINDINGS: LIBRARY INDEPENDENT VARIABLES

While the type of academic library does not cause a better performance, there is some relationship as indicated by the significant difference found in effectiveness among the four types of institutions. The best performance score was obtained by the university libraries, which would also be expected to have more books and more staff. There may be elements in addition to library classification that contributed to the differences in effectiveness. The findings presented in this chapter investigate these other elements as they pertain to the third major research question of this study:

> Is there a direct relationship between the number of correct responses and certain descriptive statistics collected by the National Center for Education Statistics, such as total operating expenditures or number of volumes in the library collection, that explains the differences among academic libraries?

As previously indicated in Chapter 2, seventy-six independent variables were selected from the 1975 Library Statistics of Colleges and Universities. The results of the tests indicated that there was a positive association between the library's performance score on the major dependent variable and fifty-one of the variables selected from Library Statistics of Colleges and Universities.

Of the seventy-six library independent variables, the number of document volumes held (variable 3) had the highest correlation with the major dependent variable (r_s = .56). This relationship is probably spurious since only twenty-one of the forty libraries indicated that they had any document

[71]

volumes and the variable was also significantly related to the
number of bookstock volumes and periodical subscriptions.
No two-year college reported any document holdings; only
three four-year colleges without graduate programs reported
documents held. The next-highest positive, significant correlation (.55) included volumes held (variable 2), shelving
capacity (variable 62), and total hours open per week (variable 64).

Stepwise multiple regression analysis was chosen to
explore the relationship between the number of correct responses and the following selected independent variables:
volumes held (variable 2), FTE number of professional staff
with a graduate degree (variable 44), total expenditures (variable 57), materials circulated (variable 58), net assignable
area (variable 61), total hours open per week (variable 64),
and FTE students (variable 67). The independent variables,
which were selected from each part of the LIBGIS survey,
represent the library's collection, staff, physical facilities,
and clients as well as services that might be related to the
major dependent variable, such as hours of opening and circulation of materials to users.

Spearman rank order correlations were computed for
the performance score on the major dependent variable and
the seven independent variables. The results of these correlations are displayed in Table 8. The two variables that
had the highest correlations with the major dependent variable were the volumes held and the hours open per week.
Total expenditures (variable 57) was the best predictor of
the other independent variables.

The rank order correlation matrix for the variables
was input into an SPSS subprogram to calculate the multiple
regression equations. When stepwise regression is used to
describe the relationship between variables, the variable
which enters the equation first is the independent variable
that accounts for the most variation in the dependent variable. On each subsequent step, the independent variable that
accounts for the greatest amount of the remaining variation
in the dependent variable will enter into the equation.

Definitions

Terms used in regression analysis that will be displayed in tables in this and subsequent chapters require some
additional explanation.

Table 8

MATRIX OF RANK ORDER CORRELATIONS FOR SEVEN LIBRARY INDEPENDENT VARIABLES*

| | | | Independent Variables | | | | | Number of |
	V2	V44	V57	V58	V61	V64	V67	Correct Responses
2. Volumes held	. . .	.90	.90	.89	.94	.90	.82	.55
44. FTE professional staff with graduate degree	.90	. . .	.93	.86	.86	.86	.87	.48
57. Total expenditures	.90	.93	. . .	.92	.86	.86	.91	.46
58. Materials circulated	.89	.86	.92	. . .	.89	.76	.89	.46
61. Net assignable area	.94	.86	.86	.89	. . .	.82	.82	.48
64. Hours open per week	.90	.86	.86	.76	.82	. . .	.74	.55
67. FTE students	.82	.87	.91	.89	.82	.74	. . .	.41
Average correlations	.89	.88	.90	.87	.86	.82	.84	.48

*N = 40; $\underline{p} \leq .01$.

R: The multiple correlation coefficient (R) represents the simple or zero-order correlation coefficient between the dependent variable and all the independent variables in the regression equation.

R^2: The squared multiple correlation coefficient represents the proportion of variation in the dependent variable that is explained by the independent variables in the regression equation. R^2 is frequently referred to as the coefficient of determination.

Adjusted R^2: Multiple R can be inflated when multiple correlation coefficients are calculated on small sample or with independent variables that were selected because they were highly correlated with the dependent variable. In these instances, it is more appropriate and conservative to use an R^2 that is corrected for this bias.

F test: The regression equation can be examined for goodness of fit on each step using the F ratio to test the null hypotheses.

Results

All academic libraries

The results of the stepwise regression for the major dependent variable and the seven selected independent variables for the forty libraries as a whole are displayed in Table 9. F ratio and tolerance level default options, which were .01 and .001 respectively, were used and all seven variables entered the equation. Hours open per week was the independent variable that accounted for the most variation in the dependent variable. Twenty-nine percent of the variance in the number of correct responses was explained by the hours open per week. When all seven variables were entered into the equation, the R^2 adjusted for bias dropped to 22 percent.

The findings indicate that the relationship between the major dependent variable and the independent variables was more than mere chance; that is, the accuracy of the response was significantly associated with the selected independent variables.

Type of institution

An initial regression equation was computed using the

Table 9

SUMMARY OF STEPWISE MULTIPLE REGRESSION ANALYSIS WITH
SEVEN LIBRARY INDEPENDENT VARIABLES FOR ALL ACADEMIC LIBRARIES

Independent Variables		r_s	R	R^2	Adjusted R^2	F Test*
64.	Hours open per week	.55	.55	.31	.29	16.74*
2.	Volumes held	.55	.56	.32	.28	8.68*
57.	Total expenditures	.46	.58	.33	.28	6.04*
61.	Net assignable area	.48	.59	.34	.27	4.58*
58.	Materials circulated	.46	.60	.36	.26	3.78*
44.	FTE professional staff with graduate degree	.48	.60	.36	.24	3.08*
67.	FTE students	.41	.60	.36	.22	2.56*

*N = 40; $\underline{p} \leq .05$.

seven selected independent variables and the type of institution. The type of institution entered the equation on the first step, which indicates that it accounted for the most variation in the major dependent variable. Thirty-two percent of the variation in the number of correct responses could be accounted for when the type of institution was ranked from two-year colleges (1) to universities (4). Since there were significant differences in effectiveness among types of institutions, separate analyses were conducted for the seven selected independent variables by the four types of institutions. The multiple regression analysis by type of institution did not display any particular pattern.

The hours open per week did have a low, positive association with the performance score for three of the four groups: two-year colleges, four-year colleges without graduate programs, and four-year colleges with graduate programs. Hours open per week had a low, negative association with the number of correct responses when the universities were separately analyzed. The hours per week variable entered the equation first for the four-year colleges with graduate programs and did not enter the equation for the two-year colleges. This pattern shows not only that hours per week is related to the other independent variables tested but also tends to indicate that once a minimum level has been reached there are few additional gains.

The substantial association between the four types of institutions and the number of correct responses ($r_s = .57$, $N = 40$, $p < .001$) was considerably reduced when controlled by either the number of volumes held ($r_s = .19$, $p > .10$) or hours open per week ($r_s = .21$, $p > .10$). This indicates that the relationship between type of institution and performance was probably spurious.

Four-year colleges without graduate programs

Regression equations were not computed for the four-year colleges without graduate programs because the number of variables being tested exceeded the number of cases available. Separate correlations were computed for each type of control and these results are displayed in Table 10.

The net assignable area had a substantial positive correlation with the number of correct answers for public four-year colleges and an identical negative correlation for private four-year colleges. Since staff in the private four-year colleges found more acceptable answers during the performance test, there is some indication that the less physical space a finite number of staff have to serve, the better the reference/ information service.

Table 10

CORRELATION BETWEEN THE NUMBER OF CORRECT RESPONSES AND SEVEN LIBRARY INDEPENDENT VARIABLES FOR FOUR-YEAR COLLEGES WITHOUT GRADUATE PROGRAMS BY TYPE OF CONTROL

Independent Variables	Type of Control	
	Public (N=10)	Private (N=10)
2. Volumes held	.15	.46
44. FTE professional staff with graduate degree	-.55	.54
57. Total expenditures	-.56	.36
58. Materials circulated	.46	.36
61. Net assignable area	.67	-.67
64. Hours open per week	.00	.82*
67. FTE students	-.20	.36

*$p \leq .05$.

Volumes held had a positive association with the number of correct responses for both the public and private four-year colleges without graduate programs. Hours open per week also showed promise as a discriminating variable since it was the only one of the seven independent variables that had a significant correlation with the performance score.

The correlation between the type of control (public or private) and the number of correct responses (r_s = .71, N = 10, p = .011) was not reduced when controlled by either hours open per week or volumes held. Obviously, the library independent variables do not adequately explain the differences in effectiveness between public and private four-year colleges without graduate programs.

Suggested Basic Levels

While the instrument used may not have been sensitive to individual performance, it had sufficient reliability to distinguish among groups. In general, the regression equations for the various classifications of academic libraries were not significant. Yet, the equation for the forty libraries as a whole was significant. This discrepancy lends support to quantitative standards that suggest minimum requirements. In this study, there appear to be certain basic levels that correspond closely with the type of institution. Small ranges within the basic levels have little or no significant effects.

For the forty libraries, two independent variables (hours open per week and volumes held) accounted for more of the variation in the major dependent variable than the other five independent variables tested.

Library volumes held

There was a progressive increase in the median number of volumes by type of institution as follows: two-year colleges (24,000), four-year colleges without graduate programs (90,000), four-year colleges with graduate programs (148,000), and universities (875,000). There was little difference in the median number of volumes between public (89,744) and private (89,352) four-year colleges without graduate programs. The volumes held by the forty libraries ranged from approximately 15,000 to over two million.

One widely used standard suggests a basic collection of 85,000 volumes.[1] A Mann-Whitney U test indicated that there were significant differences in the number of correct responses between libraries with less than and more than 85,000 volumes (U = 66.0, $p \leq$ .001).

As indicated in Table 11, libraries that held more than

85,000 volumes were more likely (57.7 percent) to give responses that were more than 50 percent correct, or six right answers to the twelve queries. Libraries with fewer than 85,000 volumes were more likely (64.3 percent) to find less than 50 percent of the correct responses.

Table 11

PERCENTAGE DISTRIBUTION OF THE PERFORMANCE SCORE: NUMBER OF CORRECT RESPONSES BY LIBRARY VOLUMES HELD IN SELECTED CATEGORIES

Correct Responses	Volumes Held (in 1,000)		Totals
	1-84	85 or more	
Less than 50%	64.3%	15.4%	32.5%
50%	28.6	26.9	27.5
More than 50%	7.1	57.7	40.0
Totals	100.0% (N=14)	100.0% (N=26)	100.0% (N=40)

These findings lend some support to the basic volume standard recommended for four-year colleges and its applicability across types of institutions. No two-year college tested had 85,000 volumes; every university had at least 85,000 volumes. Only four of the twenty four-year colleges tested had fewer than 85,000 volumes. The two private four-year colleges that had more than 50 percent of the responses correct also had more than 85,000 volumes. The best performance in the public four-year colleges without graduate programs was 50 percent correct. This library also had more than 85,000 volumes.

The number of volumes in the library collection correlated significantly with the major dependent variable and was an excellent measure of the other six selected independent variables (see Table 8). Some volume minimums should be suggested in reference and library quantitative standards.

Library hours per week

There was a progressive increase in the median number of hours open per week by type of institution from two-year colleges (65.0) to universities (98.0). There was little difference in the median number of hours open per week between public (80) and private (77) four-year colleges without graduate programs.

A standard once widely used suggested that two- and four-year colleges be open sixty hours per week and university libraries be open at least eighty hours per week.[2] A Mann-Whitney U test indicated a significant difference in the number of correct responses between libraries open less than or more than eighty hours per week ($U = 88.5$, $\underline{p} \leq .01$).

Table 12

PERCENTAGE DISTRIBUTION OF THE PERFORM-ANCE SCORE: NUMBER OF CORRECT RESPONSES BY LIBRARY HOURS PER WEEK IN SELECTED CATEGORIES

Correct Responses	Hours per Week		Totals
	1-79	80 or more	
Less than 50%	56.3%	16.7%	32.5%
50%	31.3	25.0	27.5
More than 50%	12.4	58.3	40.0
Totals	100.0% (N=16)	100.0% (N=24)	100.0% (N=40)

As indicated in Table 12, libraries that were open more than eight hours per week were more likely (58.3 percent) to find more than 50 percent of the correct responses. In contrast, libraries open less than eight hours per week were more likely (56.3 percent) to find less than 50 percent of the correct responses.

It should be pointed out that all the academic libraries in this sample, which were once accredited by the Southern Association criteria, were open more than sixty hours per week. Although the standard is no longer used, the findings lend some support to the recommendation that libraries be open at least eighty hours per week. No two-year college was open eighty hours per week; every university was open at least eighty hours. Only six of the twenty four-year colleges were open less than eighty hours per week. No significant difference was found on the number of correct responses and the two categories of hours open in separate analyses for public and private four-year colleges without graduate programs. The number of hours open per week was more strongly related to the number of correct responses than the independent variables concerned with collection size and staff (see Table 8).

While libraries with more staff and a larger student enrollment are open more hours per week, the number of hours open is probably additionally a good proxy measure of the library's commitment to reference/information and other services. Since the number of hours open per week was also the independent variable that had the highest correlation with the dependent variable in Childers's study, it would seem advisable for future standards writers to include some suggested minimum requirements regarding hours of service.

6.

FINDINGS: REFERENCE INDEPENDENT VARIABLES

The results of the survey constructed by the investigator that collected the independent variables pertaining to reference/information services from the academic libraries tested in this study are discussed in this chapter. The findings address the fourth research question:

Is there a direct relationship between the number of correct responses and selected reference policies, procedures, and statistics, such as compliance with the "Developmental Guidelines," referral of unanswered reference questions to a senior staff member, and number of volumes in the reference collection, that explains the differences among academic libraries?

Since the findings are dependent upon the instrument used to collect them, the reliability and validity of the questionnaire are discussed first. Next, the results are detailed by survey section, and the performance test is compared with the variables pertaining to reference services and library operations for the purpose of suggesting basic minimums.

The Instrument

The methods and procedures used to construct and pretest the questionnaire, collect the data, and analyze the data were discussed in Chapter 2. The final instrument (presented in Appendix C) had over a 90-percent return rate. The responses on the first three general, numeric sections of the survey were tested for reliability using the split-half relia-

[82]

bility method. The odd items constituted the first half of the questionnaire and the even items constituted the second half.

The reliability coefficient for the survey as a whole was .73 for the fourteen respondents who answered all fifty-five numeric questions. When the survey sections were separately tested, the results ranged from .67 on the General Information section to .88 on the "Developmental Guidelines" section; therefore, the survey does have internal consistency. As discussed previously, a reliability coefficient of .50 or .60 is probably adequate for distinguishing group performance, which was the intent in this study.

Validity

Item discrimination indices were computed by calculating the Spearman rank order correlation between the responses on each question and the summed responses on that section of the questionnaire. The item discrimination indices, as detailed in Tables A, B, and C in Appendix F indicate that the survey had internal validity, in that most items correlated at the .05 level or better within their questionnaire section.

While most of the survey items had internal validity, very few had validity when compared with the external criterion effectiveness on the performance test. Only the summed statistics questions in the Background Information section had a significant correlation with the number of correct responses.

Respondents

Survey questions 56 through 60 were included to gather background information on the individuals responsible for the delivery of reference/information services in the Southeast. The typical respondent to the survey was a female who had a master's degree in library science and an undergraduate degree in a major related to language or literature. History was the most frequently mentioned single subject major with twelve responses, or 30.8 percent of the thirty-nine respondents. Only one respondent had an undergraduate major that reflected a science background: a triple major in history, geography, and geology.

In addition to their library science degree, thirteen respondents had done work beyond the bachelor's degree in another subject. Two of these had a doctorate; eleven had a second master's or other advanced work.

Thirty-four respondents answered question 60, which requested information regarding membership in selected professional organizations. Most individuals who answered this question mentioned membership in at least two organizations; one respondent mentioned six. The individuals responsible for the delivery of reference/information services in this sample appear to be more locally or regionally oriented in their professional activities than nationally oriented. Fifty-nine percent of the respondents who answered question 60 indicated membership in their state library association; 48.7 percent indicated membership in the Southeastern Library Association (SELA). In contrast, only 41 percent of the thirty-four respondents indicated membership in the American Library Association (ALA).

No respondent indicated membership in the American Society for Information Science (ASIS) which may partly explain why only three library staff members found the acceptable answer to query 6, which requested the current ASIS president. A Spearman rank order correlation was calculated between the responses on survey questions 55, 60A, and query 11. The correlation was not significant between the number of ALA members (question 55) and the number of correct answers on query 11. The fact that the individual responsible for the delivery of reference services was a member of ALA (question 60A) did correlate significantly with the number of ALA members in question 55 (r_s = .73, N = 37, p = .001) as well as the number of FTE professional staff engaged in reference/information services in question 46 (r_s = .74, N = 37, p = .001).

The respondents who mentioned membership in two ALA divisions were significantly different by type of institution. Respondents in universities or four-year colleges with graduate programs were more likely to mention membership in the Reference and Adult Services Division (RASD, question 60B) or the Association of College and Research Libraries (ACRL, question 60C). These two aspects of question 60 were the only responses on the respondents' background (questions 56 through 60) that had a significant, positive correlation with the number of correct responses. RASD membership and ACRL membership had identical rank order correlations of .30, which were significant at .032 for the thirty-nine libraries tested.

No significant associations were found between public and private four-year colleges without graduate programs or when the type of institution was controlled and a Spearman rank order correlation was computed between the responses on the membership questions and the number of correct responses.

The library's size and/or type of institution obviously influenced the correlations; one cannot conclude that performance will improve if the individual responsible for the delivery of reference/information services is a member of RASD or ACRL. In general, the responses on the questions regarding the respondents' background bore little or no relationship to performance on fact-type queries asked via telephone.

"Developmental Guidelines"

Questions 1 through 30 of the survey were adapted from RASD's "Developmental Guidelines." Respondents were asked to indicate how each statement reflected the reference/ information services in their library using a five-point response scale that ranged from "not at all" (1) to "completely" (5). Most respondents (41.8 percent of all responses) indicated that the statements adapted from the "Developmental Guidelines" reflected the reference/information services in their libraries "to a great extent" or "completely." Thirty-one percent felt that the statements reflected their reference/ information services "not at all" or "to a little extent"; 27.2 percent answered "to some extent."

A Kruskal-Wallis one-way analysis of variance by ranks indicated that there was no significant difference on the total Guidelines score or the scores by Guidelines section among the four types of institutions or between public and private four-year colleges without graduate programs. Table 13 presents the correlation matrix for the "Developmental Guidelines" as a whole and by section with the number of correct responses and other selected variables for the academic libraries as a whole.

While the rank order correlations between the Guidelines and its sections are positive and significant, the scores

Table 13

RANK ORDER CORRELATION MATRIX FOR THE
"DEVELOPMENTAL GUIDELINES" AND SELECTED VARIABLES

	P. S.		Serv.		Envir.		Per.	
	N	r_s	N	r_s	N	r_s	N	r_s
Performance score Number of correct responses	. . .	. . .						
Service score (Ques. 1-16)	32	-.23	. . .	. . .				
Environment score (Ques. 17-21)	37	-.14	31	.40*	. . .	. . .		
Personnel score (Ques. 21-27)	37	.18	32	.42*	36	.35*	. . .	. . .
Evaluation score (Ques. 28-30)	38	-.11	32	.55*	37	.32*	37	.55*
Guidelines score (Ques. 1-30)	31	-.20	31	.89*	31	.61*	31	.68*
Volumes held, library (LIBGIS V. 2)	40	.55*	32	-.18	37	-.12	37	-.02
Volumes held, reference (Ques. 52)	34	.67*	28	.07	32	-.13	32	.30
Materials circulated (LIBGIS V. 28)	40	.46*	32	-.03	37	-.13	37	-.06
Hours open per week (LIBGIS V. 64)	40	.55*	32	-.17	37	-.14	38	-.20

*$p \leq .05$.

Eval.		Guide.		Vols. Lib.		Vols. Ref.		Circ.		Hrs/Wk	
N	r_s	N	r_s	N	r_s	N	r_s	N	r_s	N	r_s
. .	. . .										
31	.79*	. .	. . .								
38	-.23	31	-.27	. .	. . .						
33	.05	27	.05	34	.72*	. .	. . .				
38	-.09	31	-.14	40	.89*	34	.57*	. .	. . .		
38	-.20	31	-.23	40	.90*	34	.75*	40	.76*	. .	. . .

have little or no association with the number of correct responses. In contrast, the number of volumes in the library, the number of volumes in the reference collection, and the hours open per week correlated positively and significantly with themselves and with the two output variables: materials circulated and number of correct responses.

Individual Guidelines questions. The correlations between the number of correct responses and the responses on the individual Guidelines questions are displayed in Appendix F. The four questions that correlated at the .05 level or less for the forty academic libraries were questions 2, 3, 15, and 23. These questions, presented in Table 14, will be separately discussed.

Twenty-eight, or 73.6 percent of the thirty-eight respondents who answered questions 2 and 3, indicated that they did not have a published reference service code available to all users. The moderate negative correlation with the number of correct responses was primarily influenced by two respondents who indicated that statements 2 and 3 reflected the reference/information service in their library "completely," yet scored only four correct responses each in the performance test. When the type of institution was controlled, the rank order correlations computed between the responses on questions 2 and 3 and the performance score were not significant at the .05 level. A published service code does not necessarily mean a poorer performance on fact-type queries. It might be more appropriate to conclude that academic libraries in this sample, regardless of type, do not have a published service code.

Question 15 was the only question in the Guidelines section of the questionnaire that had responses that differed significantly by type of institution. On question 15, which dealt with the availability of frequently used materials in multiple copies, the mean rank of the responses from the two-year colleges was higher and significantly different from the mean rank of the responses in the other types of institutions. As indicated in Table 14, the responses to question 15 correlated significantly in a negative direction with the performance score primarily because the two-year colleges had fewer correct answers on the twelve queries. No significant correlations between the responses to question 15 and the performance score were found when the type of institution was controlled or for public and private four-year colleges without graduate programs.

Table 14

RANK ORDER CORRELATION MATRIX FOR THE INDIVIDUAL "DEVELOPMENTAL GUIDELINES" QUESTIONS THAT WERE ASSOCIATED SIGNIFICANTLY WITH THE NUMBER OF CORRECT RESPONSES

	P.S.		SQ2		SQ3		SQ15		SQ23		Guide.	
	N	r_s	N	r_s	N	r_s	N	r_s	N	r_s	N	r_s
Performance score Number of correct responses	.	.										
Survey questions												
2. Service code published	38	− .33*	.	.								
3. Service code details	38	− .32*	38	.99*	.	.						
15. Multiple copies	39	− .29*	38	− .02	38	− .03	.	.				
23. Librarian available	39	.30*	38	.02	38	.06	39	.03	.	.		
Guidelines score	31	− .20	31	.48*	31	.49*	31	.42*	31	.45*	.	.

*$\underline{p} \leq .05.$

Question 23 was the only item in the Guidelines section that correlated significantly in a positive direction with the performance score for the academic libraries as a whole. While the Kruskal-Wallis one-way analysis of variance did not indicate a significant difference by library type, a large percentage of respondents in four-year colleges and universities (93.7 percent) indicated that they had a professional librarian available during the hours the library was open either "completely" or "to a great extent." In contrast, only 50 percent of the respondents in two-year colleges and four-year colleges without graduate programs indicated that statement 23 reflected the reference/information services in their library either "completely" or "to a great extent." There was a significant correlation between the responses on question 23 and the number of hours per typical week the library offered reference/information services in question 48 (r_s = .37, N = 38, p = .01).

Question 7 was the only Guidelines question that exhibited significant differences between public and private four-year colleges without graduate programs. Respondents from the public colleges were more likely to indicate that bibliographical and other informational access guides were developed in their library either "to a great extent" or "completely" (three, or 60 percent) than respondents in private four-year colleges without graduate programs (0 percent). There was no significant correlation between the responses on question 7 and the number of correct responses in the performance test by type of control or for the four-year colleges without graduate programs as a whole.

In general, the responses on the "Developmental Guidelines" bore little relationship to the major dependent variable in this study. Additionally, there is some indication that certain guidelines lack internal consistency. While it is possible that the guidelines measure some aspect of reference/information services that was not measured by accuracy of response to fact-type queries asked via telephone, it should be of serious concern to the profession when the responses also show no association with other standard measures, such as the number of volumes in the reference collection.

General information

The thirty-nine respondents indicated how each of the fourteen statements in the General Information section of the survey related to reference/information services in their library on a five-point scale that ranged from "never" (1) to "always" (5). The responses to questions 35, 42, 43, and 44 were reversed for scoring.

The responses on the individual statements and the summed responses on the General Information sectior questions as a whole (31 through 44) did not correlate significantly with the performance score at the .05 level.

Background statistics

On the third and final section of the survey, the respondents provided background information on their library and themselves. Since the background of the respondents was discussed above, this section will only present the findings on statistics pertaining to reference/information services (questions 45 through 55).

As indicated in Appendix F, eight of the eleven numeric background questions correlated significantly with the number of correct responses. The variables with the highest correlations included number of reference volumes (survey question 52, r_s = .67), hours of library service (survey question 48, r_s = .62), and hours of reference service (survey question 49, r_s = .54).

Hours. The number of library hours per week was collected via LIBGIS (variable 64) and in the survey of academic libraries (question 48). The survey also requested the number of hours per typical week that reference/information service was offered to users (question 49). Table 15 displays the intercorrelations between these three variables concerning hours of service and the number of correct responses.

The correlation between the major dependent variable and the hours of service in Table 15 differs from that shown in Chapter 5 because missing values are now being deleted listwise. In listwise deletion, if an observation is not present on one of the variables being tested, the case is not examined on any of the variables.

Library hours had higher correlations with the performance score than the reference hours. Since the 1975 LIBGIS "hours per week" and the 1977 survey "hours per week" had a high positive correlation (r_s = .91), confidence can be placed in the reliability and validity of the responses on the other survey items.

Table 15

MATRIX OF RANK ORDER CORRELATIONS FOR THE MAJOR DEPENDENT VARIABLE AND INDEPENDENT VARIABLES CONCERNING LIBRARY/REFERENCE HOURS OF SERVICE*

	P. S.	V64	SQ48	SQ49
Performance score Number of correct responses	. . .			
Hours per week, library (LIBGIS, V. 64)	.65	. . .		
Hours per week, library (Survey question 48)	.62	.91	. . .	
Hours per week, reference (Survey question 49)	.54	.68	.81	. . .

*Missing values deleted listwise; N = 38, $\underline{p} \leq .001$.

Reference volumes. The number of volumes in the library had a stronger correlation with the number of correct responses than the number of volumes in the reference collection (see Table 16). This result was not expected; however, the queries asked during the performance test did not have to be answered using a reference book. Additionally, it should be pointed out that the number of volumes in the reference collection had more rank order ties and probably less discriminating power than the number of volumes in the library. The number of ready reference volumes was correlated with the time measures used in Chapter 3. No significant correlations were found.

In general, the majority of the statistics concerning

reference/information services were found to relate positively and significantly to the performance score: number of correct responses. When the reference statistics and similar variables concerning overall library operations were compared, the library independent variables had a slightly higher correlation with the number of correct responses.

Table 16

MATRIX OF RANK ORDER CORRELATIONS FOR THE MAJOR DEPENDENT VARIABLE AND INDEPENDENT VARIABLES CONCERNING LIBRARY/REFERENCE VOLUMES HELD[a]

	P. S.	V2	SQ52	SQ53
Performance score Number of correct responses	. . .			
Volumes, library (LIBGIS, V. 2)	.68	. . .		
Volumes, reference (Survey question 52)	.67	.73	. . .	
Volumes, ready reference (Survey question 53)	.28[b]	.65	.32	. . .

[a] Missing values deleted listwise, N = 33, $p \leq .05$ unless otherwise indicated.
[b] $.05 > p < .10$.

Independent Variables and Effectiveness

Multiple regression analysis was used to examine selected independent variables pertaining to library and reference services and their relationship to the performance score: number of correct responses. The colinearity between the variables was taken into account by using stepwise regression so that the variables entered the equation as independent predictors of effectiveness (the criterion). Twelve library and reference independent variables were selected from the LIBGIS data and the survey of academic library reference/information services. The five reference independent variables selected were as follows: volumes, reference (question 52); librarians, reference (question 46); questions, reference (question 51); questions, directional (question 50); and hours, reference (question 49). Only twenty-five of the forty respondents provided data on all five reference independent variables.

The seven library independent variables, previously discussed, were also analyzed for the twenty-five libraries using listwise deletion. The library independent variables were as follows: volumes, library or volumes held (variable 2); librarians, library or professional staff with a graduate degree (variable 44); total expenditures (variable 57); materials circulated (variable 58); net assignable area (variable 61); hours, library or hours open per week (variable 64); and FTE students (variable 67).

A summary of the stepwise multiple regression analysis is displayed in Table 17. While the F test indicated that the multiple R for the first ten variables was significantly different from zero, the adjusted R^2 did not increase after the first two variables entered the equation. Fifty-six percent of the variation in the number of correct responses was explained by the following two variables: volumes, reference and hours, reference.

It is interesting to note that the reference independent variables pertaining to volumes and hours entered the equation before the library independent variables pertaining to volumes and hours. For the twenty-five libraries on which data were available on both reference and library independent variables, the reference independent variables seemed to explain more of the variation in the major dependent variable. The hours of library service did not enter the equation until the ninth step even though it had a higher correlation with the number of correct responses ($r_s = .67$) than the number of hours of reference/information services ($r_s = .64$).

Type of institution

The Spearman rank order correlations between the number of correct responses and the twelve independent variables by type of institution were computed for each of the four types of institutions. The best measure of the major dependent var-

Table 17

SUMMARY OF STEPWISE MULTIPLE REGRESSION
ANALYSIS WITH LIBRARY AND REFERENCE
INDEPENDENT VARIABLES FOR ALL ACADEMIC
LIBRARIES

Independent Variables	r_s	R	R^2	Adjusted R^2	F Test*
Volumes, reference	.70	.70	.49	.47	21.81*
Hours, reference	.64	.76	.58	.56	15.23*
Net assignable area	.61	.77	.59	.55	9.96*
Librarians, reference	.45	.78	.60	.56	7.60*
Volumes, library	.66	.78	.61	.55	5.95*
Librarians, library	.66	.79	.62	.55	4.89*
Questions, directional	.39	.79	.63	.55	4.12*
Questions, reference	.48	.81	.65	.56	3.78*
Hours, library	.67	.81	.66	.56	3.31*
FTE students	.51	.82	.67	.55	2.83*
Materials circulated	.58	.82	.67	.54	2.43
Total expenditures	.60	.82	.68	.53	2.08

*Missing values deleted listwise; N = 25, $p \leq .05$.

iable in two-year colleges was the number of FTE students
enrolled (r_s = .85). The number of volumes in the reference collection had the highest correlation with the number
of correct responses for four-year colleges without graduate
programs (r_s = .61) and universities (r_s = .84). Hours of
reference service had the highest correlation with the number of correct responses for four-year colleges with graduate programs.

While the pattern of association is somewhat irregu-
lar, the number of volumes in the reference collection was
the only independent variable that had a positive association
with the major dependent variable in all four types of librar-

ies. The relationship ranged from very strong (.84) for the universities to negligible (.06) for the four-year colleges with graduate programs where only four cases were available for analysis. The number of hours per typical week that reference services were offered was also a good measure since it had a positive association with the number of correct responses in three of the four types of institutions.

The correlation between the number of correct responses and the type of institution was substantial (r_s = .67, N = 25, p < .001) when the libraries were ranked sequentially from two-year colleges (1) to universities (4). The correlation was no longer significant when controlled by the number of volumes in the reference collection (r_s = .25, p > .10). When the hours of reference/information services per week was used as a control, the partial correlation was still significant (r_s = .38, p = .032). The fact that the strength of the association was considerably reduced indicates that the relationship between the number of correct responses and the type of institution was spurious.

Four-year colleges without graduate programs

Rank order correlations were separately computed for the four-year colleges without graduate programs. The only pattern apparent was that the number of volumes in the reference collection had a positive correlation with the number of correct responses in both public (r_s = .32) and private (r_s = .63) four-year colleges without graduate programs; this correlation was much stronger for the privately controlled institutions.

The substantial correlation between the number of correct responses and the type of control (r_s = .67, N = 8, p = .033) was considerably reduced when controlled by the number of reference volumes held (r_s = .40, p > .10). The correlation was still substantial but no longer significant when controlled by the hours of reference service per week (r_s = .64, p = .061). These findings indicate that the relationship between the type of control and performance for the four-year colleges without graduate programs is probably spurious.

Suggested Basic Levels

As pointed out in Chapter 5, when the forty academic

libraries were considered, the two library independent variables that explained the most variation in the dependent variables were hours open per week and volumes held. Observations on both reference and library independent variables were
examined for twenty-five libraries. For these cases, the reference independent variables were generally more closely related to the number of correct responses. The two reference
independent variables that accounted for the most variation in
the dependent variable were the number of volumes in the
reference collection and the number of hours per week that
reference/information services were offered. The fact that
the findings for the library independent variables were replicated with the reference independent variables provides further evidence that hours of service and volumes in the collection are related to reference performance as measured by accuracy of response to fact-type queries.

The raw and rank order data for the number of volumes in the reference collection and the hours per week reference services are displayed in Appendix G along with the
number of correct responses, the type of institution, and the
type of control. Summary statistics describing the two reference independent variables by type of institution are presented in Appendices G and H. These data were examined
to locate possible basic levels for future standards.

Reference volumes held

There was a progressive increase in the median number of reference volumes by type of institution as follows:
two-year colleges (2,021), four-year colleges without graduate programs (5,050), four-year colleges with graduate programs (9,900), and universities (20,000). There was also a
difference in the median number of reference volumes between
public (3,700) and private (7,400) four-year colleges without
graduate programs.

After his obtrusive study of public libraries, Powell
concluded that there was a causal relationship between reference collection size and the percent of reference questions
answered correctly. He also found that the relationship between the two variables was curvilinear with a diminishing
return noticeable once a reference collection reached about
3,500 volumes. A scattergram was generated for similar
variables in this study. The scattergram for the number of
correct responses and the number of volumes in the reference
collection did not indicate a curvilinear relationship.

The discrepancy between the findings of this investigation and Powell's study can be attributed to differences in methodology and the libraries sampled. The percentage of correct responses was slightly higher in Powell's obtrusive study (59 percent) than in this unobtrusive study (50 percent). The fifty-one public libraries tested by Powell had a median of 2,205 reference volumes; fourteen libraries had less than 1,000 reference volumes; and only three had more than 10,000 volumes.[1] In contrast, the twenty-five academic libraries analyzed in this study had a median of 6,500 volumes; only one library had less than 1,000 volumes; and eight libraries had more than 10,000 volumes. There is some evidence to indicate that the public library staff members who knew that they were being tested exploited their smaller reference collections to a greater extent than the academic library staff members who did not know that they were being tested.

The academic library reference collections ranged from 350 to 26,500 volumes. As indicated by the raw data in Appendix G, the library with 350 reference volumes had less than 50 percent of the responses correct. A library needed 1,000 or more volumes before six correct responses were given (50 percent of the twelve queries). At least 7,000 volumes were held before more than 50 percent of the responses were correct. The library with the highest number of correct responses (nine, or 75 percent) was also the library with the largest reference collection (26,500 volumes). The relationship between the number of reference volumes and the number of correct responses measured unobtrusively is more linear than that found by Powell; however, 3,500 volumes could serve as one cutoff point.

As indicated in Table 18, no library with fewer than 3,500 volumes in the reference collection gave more than 50 percent of the correct responses. No library with more than 10,000 volumes failed to find 50 percent or more of the correct answers.

A Kruskal-Wallis one-way analysis of variance indicated that there was a significant difference among the three categories of reference volumes and the number of correct responses ($H = 16.20$, $N = 25$, $p < .001$). Subsequent Mann-Whitney U tests indicated that the number of correct responses was different at the .05 level of significance between libraries with more than 10,000 volumes and the libraries with 3,500 to 9,999 volumes as well as the libraries with fewer than 3,500 reference volumes. The median number of correct responses by category of reference volumes

Table 18

PERCENTAGE DISTRIBUTION OF THE PERFORMANCE SCORE:
NUMBER OF CORRECT RESPONSES BY REFERENCE VOLUMES HELD IN SELECTED CATEGORIES

Correct Responses	Volumes Held			Totals
	1-3,499	3,500-9,999	10,000 or more	
Less than 50%	55.6%	37.5%	0.0%	32.0%
50%	44.4	37.5	25.0	36.0
More than 50%	0.0	25.0	75.0	32.0
Totals	100.0% (N=9)	100.0% (N=8)	100.0% (N=8)	100.0% (N=25)

are as follows: fewer than 3,500 volumes (5.0), 3,500-9,999 (5.8), 10,000 or more (7.5).

The number of volumes in the reference collection is highly associated with the accuracy of response to fact-type queries, as indicated by this investigation and in Powell's study of public libraries. Minimum levels for this variable should be suggested in standards for reference service. The number of reference volumes should be collected by LIBGIS on a regular basis to facilitate the formulation of such standards.

Reference hours per week

There were differences by type of institution in the median hours of reference service per week as follows: two-year colleges (65.0), four-year colleges without graduate programs (60.5), four-year colleges with graduate programs (81.0), and universities (85.2). The lower median hours per week reference service for the four-year colleges without graduate programs can be attributed largely to the staff in public four-year colleges without graduate programs (median 42.5) rather than the staff in private four-year colleges without graduate programs, who not only did better in the performance test but also offered a median of 71.5 hours per week reference service.

Table 19 displays three selected categories of hours of reference service by three percentage categories of the number of correct responses. Libraries that offered less than seventy hours per week reference service were less likely to find 50 percent or more of the correct responses. No library offering eighty or more hours of reference service per week failed to find at least 50 percent of the correct answers.

The Kruskal-Wallis one-way analysis of variance by ranks indicated that there was a significant difference in the number of correct responses among the three categories of hours of reference service (H = 10.45, N = 25, $\underline{p}$ = .005). The subsequent Mann-Whitney U tests indicated that there were differences in the number of correct responses significant at the .05 level between libraries offering less than seventy hours and libraries offering reference services eighty or more hours per week. While the differences were not significant at the .05 level, Table 19 indicates that there

Table 19

PERCENTAGE DISTRIBUTION OF THE PERFORMANCE
SCORE: NUMBER OF CORRECT RESPONSES BY
REFERENCE HOURS PER WEEK IN SELECTED
CATEGORIES

Correct Responses	Hours per Week			
	1-69	70-79	80 or more	Totals
Less than 50%	60.0%	33.3%	0.0%	32.0%
50%	40.0	33.3	33.3	36.0
More than 50%	0.0	33.3	66.7	32.0
Totals	100.0% (N=10)	100.0% (N=6)	100.0% (N=9)	100.0% (N=25)

were differences in a linear direction among the other categories of hours of reference service. The median number of correct responses by categories of reference hours were as follows: less than seventy hours (5.0), seventy to seventy-nine hours per week (6.0), and eighty or more hours (7.3).

The raw data displayed (see Appendix G) also point out that libraries offered reference services at least seventy hours per week before over 50 percent of the answers were correct. The library offering the longest hours of reference service (100 hours per week) was also the library with the largest number of correct responses (nine) and the largest number of volumes in the reference collection (26,500).

It should be pointed out that the number of volumes in the reference collection had a substantial, positive correlation with the number of hours of reference service per week (r_s = .56, N = 25, p = .002). There are indications that once basic levels are achieved the number of hours per week that reference services are offered may be serving as a proxy indication of the library's commitment to reference/information services and/or the staff's ability to exploit the reference collection. All libraries that answered more than

50 percent of the queries correctly were open at least eighty hours per week and offered reference services over 70 percent of these hours. The true nature of the relationship between these variables is left to future researchers.

7.
SUMMARY, CONCLUSIONS, COMMENTS

The purpose of this investigation was to explore the effectiveness of reference/information services in academic libraries using unobtrusive measures. The study examined the responses to fact-type queries asked via telephone and various independent variables including classifications of academic libraries, descriptive statistics concerning library and reference operations, and other key aspects of reference services.

Since existing conditions were surveyed, the general research method was viewed as descriptive. The results of this study may not be able to be generalized due to certain assumptions and limitations that pertain primarily to the population and the investigation technique. As indicated in Chapter 2, the population for this study was limited to 361 institutions in nine southeastern states that were not specialty colleges, had at least two staff members with graduate degrees, and that did not have a predominantly black student body. A disproportionate stratified random sample was drawn from the 361 libraries that constituted the population. Observations on twelve fact-type queries from forty academic libraries were subjected to final analysis.

The instruments used in the study included observations on fact-type queries asked via telephone, the National Center for Education Statistics Library General Information Survey (LIBGIS) data from 1975, and a questionnaire constructed by the investigator to collect independent variables related to reference services, which had a 94.9-percent return rate. The data were collected to address four research questions:

[103]

[104] Marcia J. Myers

1. Can reference/information services in academic libraries be unobtrusively measured by performance on fact-type queries asked via telephone?

2. Are there differences in effectiveness among academic libraries classified as to type of control and/or type of institution?

3. Is there a direct relationship between the number of correct responses and certain descriptive statistics collected by the National Center for Education Statistics, such as total operating expenditures or number of volumes in the library, that explains the differences among academic libraries?

4. Is there a direct relationship between the number of correct responses and selected reference policies, procedures, and statistics, such as compliance with the "Developmental Guidelines," referral of unanswered questions to a senior staff member, or number of volumes in the reference collection, that explains the differences among academic libraries?

The four research questions were answered affirmatively, but with some qualifications that will be discussed below.

Findings

The queries and unobtrusive measures

The results of the performance test used in this study appear to be reliable and valid. The reliability coefficient of the instrument was .58, which is sufficient to distinguish group performance. There is 95-percent confidence that the 361 academic libraries in nine southeastern states would have given the correct responses to the twelve query performance test 49 percent of the time ($\pm$ 1.5 percent). The findings of this study were similar to the results of previous studies on selectively matched individual queries and in the percentage of correct responses on the overall performance test.

The instrument became obtrusive first in the smaller academic libraries. No evidence of exposure or reactivity of the instrument was found in four-year colleges with graduate programs or in universities.

Prior to final analysis, fourteen libraries were eliminated and/or replaced. This principle of substitution is widely used, especially in quota sampling. No significant difference was found between the replaced libraries and their alternates on the major dependent variable, accuracy of response.

Over 50 percent of the library staff required at least one call back before a response was received. While some instantaneous acceptable answers were given, library staff members needed about three minutes to give the correct response. The median search time before suggesting a call back was approximately four minutes.

Performance was poorest on queries that could not be easily answered with the usual tools. There was evidence that even when the library owned the appropriate source, staff members either did not consult, did not know how to use, or misinterpreted the information given in the source. Staff members in the libraries tested volunteered the source of their response only 26.8 percent of the time, which is contrary to typical library school training.

Library classifications

The observations on twelve queries were totaled to create performance scores for forty libraries. The performance scores on thirteen dependent variables were used to examine the differences in effectiveness among academic libraries classified as to type of institution and/or type of control.

There were no real differences in effectiveness when the academic libraries were classified only by type of control (public or private). There was a significant difference in effectiveness when the libraries were classified by type of institution.

The median number of correct responses progressively increased from two-year colleges (5.0), four-year colleges without (5.5) and with graduate programs (6.5), to the universities (7.5). The two-year colleges had significantly fewer correct responses than the four-year colleges with graduate programs or the universities; the four-year colleges without graduate programs had significantly fewer correct responses than the universities.

Institutions with graduate programs (four-year colleges with graduate programs and universities) were more likely to volunteer the source of their response. While there appeared to be some relationship between the volunteering of the source used and the accuracy of the response, staff members infrequently volunteered the source of their response regardless of the type of institution.

There were few differences in effectiveness when the academic libraries were classified by type of institution and type of control. The number of correct responses was only significantly different between public and private four-year colleges without graduate programs. The staff in the private four-year colleges without graduate programs were more effective but slightly less efficient since they would have caused the patron a longer time delay before response than the staff in public four-year colleges without graduate programs.

The findings on the major dependent variable did not appear to be influenced by peripheral independent variables, such as the state in which the library was located or the hour and/or day of the week of the initial telephone call.

Library independent variables

Seventy-six independent variables pertaining to library operations, selected from the LIBGIS data, were separately correlated with the number of correct responses; fifty-one had a significant, positive association. Further analysis was conducted using stepwise multiple regression and seven variables selected to represent the library's clients, collections, professional staff, physical facilities, and services that might be related to the major dependent variable, such as hours of opening and circulation of materials to users.

The two library independent variables that explained the most variation (28 percent) in the number of correct responses were hours open per week and volumes held. Libraries with 85,000 or more volumes or open eighty or more hours per week performed significantly better than libraries with fewer than 85,000 volumes or open less than eighty hours per week.

The substantial correlation between the four types of institutions and the number of correct responses was not significant when controlled by either hours open per week or volumes held. The two variables did not adequately explain the difference in the number of correct responses between public and private four-year colleges without graduate programs.

Reference independent variables

The responses on the "Developmental Guidelines" section, the General Information section, and the background questions on the respondent bore little or no relationship to the number of correct responses. Nine of the eleven reference statistics questions had a positive, significant association with the number of correct responses.

When twelve independent variables pertaining to library and reference statistics were subjected to further analysis, the number of volumes in the reference collection and the hours of reference service per week were the two variables that accounted for the most variation (56 percent) in the number of correct responses. The substantial correlations between the number of correct responses and the four types of institutions as well as between the public and private four-year colleges without graduate programs were considerably reduced when controlled by the number of volumes in the reference collection and the hours of reference service.

Libraries with fewer than 3, 500 volumes in the reference collection had a lower median number of correct responses on the twelve query performance test (5. 0) than libraries with 3, 500-9, 999 volumes (5. 8) or more than 10, 000 volumes (7. 5). Libraries that offered less than seventy hours of reference service per week also had a lower median number of correct responses (5. 0) than libraries offering seventy to seventy-nine hours (6. 0) or eighty or more hours of reference service per week (7. 3).

Conclusions

During this study, reference/information services in academic libraries were successfully measured unobtrusively. The primary conclusion is that there are differences in effectiveness among classifications of academic libraries as measured by the number of correct responses to fact-type queries asked via telephone. These differences in effectiveness among types of institutions can be attributed to the size of the library rather than its classification per se. The substantial association between the number of correct responses and the four types of institutions was considered spurious since it was greatly reduced when controlled by other independent variables such as the number of volumes in the reference collection.

The reasons for the significant differences in effectiveness between public and private four-year colleges without graduate programs were not completely clear; however, the substantial association was also greatly reduced when controlled by the number of volumes in the reference collection. In general, reference/information services are not influenced by the type of control (public or private).

In this study, four-year colleges without graduate programs performed closer to the two-year colleges, and four-year colleges with graduate programs seemed more similar to the universities. It is doubtful that the same quantitative standards should continue to be used to evaluate the two types of four-year colleges.

It should be of serious concern to the profession that the "Developmental Guidelines" bore little relationship to actual reference/information performance. Question 23 was the only item from the "Guidelines" that was positively and significantly related to the number of correct responses.

The findings of this study indicate that quantitative standards can and should be developed for reference services that presently lack accuracy. The fact that the findings for the library independent variables were replicated with the reference independent variables provides strong evidence that hours of service and volumes in the collection are associated with the accuracy of response to fact-type queries. Minimum levels should be suggested in standards for reference service. Statistics on at least these two reference variables should be collected on a regular basis by LIBGIS to facilitate the formation of such standards. A bank of test reference questions, established on a national level, could be used to validate the standards.

Independent variables, such as hours of service and volumes held, were more closely related to the accuracy of the response than variables concerned with staff. This finding supports the contention that once certain basic levels are reached it is not absolute staffing numbers that influence performance but rather the ability of the staff to exploit the collections. This contention has implications, which are detailed in the next section, for librarians, library administrators, and teachers of library science.

Implications and Discussion

Library and reference/information service administrators should consider unobtrusively testing their staff to ascertain the real level of reference service being provided to users. Certain staff members encountered during this study should not have had a high evaluation under any objective performance appraisal system. Additionally, they would have benefited from some additional instruction in proper reference procedures.

As part of her extensive literature review (cited in Chapter 1), Nice M. de Figueiredo developed a typology of errors in reference work that also provides helpful suggestions for error prevention. Her recommendations for remedial actions should be studied by those responsible for in-service training programs, continuing education courses, and library school curricula as well as by the practicing reference librarian.

There are indications that library staff use the most accessible sources and seldom search beyond their library's resources. If this is so, it has some bearing on the physical arrangement of reference collections and reference service areas, as well as serious implications for the philosophy behind the establishment of reference/information networks.

If academic libraries can answer fact-type queries correctly only about 50 percent of the time, they should be emphasizing other aspects of reference services that, one hopes, they perform better, such as readers' advisory service, guidance, and teaching. Additionally, while it has not been established that patrons really care about the accuracy of the response, they continue to use our less than perfect reference/information services. Perhaps patrons know that the librarian performs better than they would in both accuracy and search time.

Since this was an exploratory study, some of these rather tentative implications require further research. Future studies will add to our relatively meager knowledge regarding the evaluation of reference services. The true value of reference performance studies will be realized eventually when it is known what reference librarians do right, what they do wrong, and how they can do better.

Appendix A

QUERY RESPONSE FORM

Library No.:
Query No.:
Score:

Library:

Location:

Telephone:

Time of initial call:

Date of initial call:

Query:

Refusal to answer (if applicable):

Call back (if required):

Date: Time (EST):   Time (CST):

Referral (if made):

If immediate answer, length of time (in minutes):

Sex of respondent: male___; female___; unable to tell___

Response:

Source (if volunteered):

Please record any other observations you have about this query to this library on the back of this form.

[111]

Appendix B

PROXY INSTRUCTIONS

The research project requires that you be thorough and exact; please record all pertinent information as accurately as possible during the telephone call or immediately following the completion of the call. If you run into any difficulties, I can be reached at 665-9687 or 685-4252.

The queries should be asked exactly as worded at the time and date indicated for each library. Some libraries are not in the Eastern Time Zone. In those cases, the fact the library is on Central Standard Time (CST) is indicated for your call back purposes. All telephone calls should be placed at the Eastern Standard Time (EST) indicated; CST (randomly assigned) have been translated into EST for your convenience.

Some libraries can be reached only through the college switchboard; others have a separate telephone number for reference assistance; and other libraries have a separate library switchboard. While attempts have been made to indicate which type of telephone number you will reach, if you are in doubt, ask if you are speaking to the reference librarian before stating the query.

If the library telephone number is not answered, try the same number the next day at the same time. If no answer is received on the second day, please notify me. It is possible that the telephone number given for the library is no longer correct.

If the library telephone number is busy, try again every fifteen minutes or so. If a library telephone number is busy in the 3 p.m.-3:30 p.m. time slot, do not attempt to call after 3:30 p.m.; call starting at 9 a.m. the next working day. After 3:30 p.m., call backs may still be completed. Please indicate the day and time that the initial call was actually placed, if they differ from those previously randomly assigned.

The library staff member answering the telephone may refuse to answer the query. If so, record the information about this refusal as completely as possible in the appropriate section on the Query Response Form.

You do not mind waiting on the telephone for an answer; however, if the library staff member wants to call you back, this is not feasible. On these call back requests, the library staff member will probably ask for your name and telephone number. Please use your preassigned name and your preassigned excuse. If the library staff member does not specify a time for calling back, you suggest one-half hour. In any case, make arrangements to call the library back at a time convenient to you both. Even a two-day delay is acceptable. Remember the time zone difference, if any, when returning a call at an agreed upon time!

The library staff member may suggest that you come into the library in person and consult certain sources. Record this information under referral. Most referrals will take place when the library staff member suggests that you telephone some other office, agency, library division, college department, or another library. Call these referrals, if they are within the library or its parent institution (university or college). You may ask the library staff member for the telephone number, if necessary. If the referral agency is outside the college or university or its library, such as a public library, note the appropriate information but do not bother to request the telephone number or call for a response.

Most library staff members will want to call you back; however, some will answer the query immediately. In those cases, record the search time in minutes and seconds. After you complete the query statement and the rationale, the library staff member will probably ask a question or two. Then, the library staff member will either ask to call you back or say something to indicate that she or he will start the search immediately, such as "OK, hold on a minute." Measure the search time from the second the library staff member indicates that the search will start immediately until she or he comes back to the telephone with a response. The response could very well be that you will have to call back. Please do not time intermediate responses and conversations with the library staff member, who might check back with you every three minutes or so. Do count the time spent away from the telephone (search time) until an answer is received, a call back is requested, or until a library staff member says the answer is unable to be found. Record the sex of the library staff member you timed by placing a check mark in the appropriate category under sex of respondent on the Query Response Form. If you are not sure that the re-

[113]

spondent actually performed the search, then make a check mark by "unable to tell."

Also, record the sex of the library staff member who recorded your original query and rationale, even though an answer was not immediately attempted, by circling the appropriate category under sex of respondent. If you are not sure of the sex of the library staff member, circle "unable to tell."

Record the response exactly as given by the library staff member. Ask her or him to repeat it or spell words if it is necessary. A rationale has been provided for most of the queries. This rationale must be given with your initial query statement. You may repeat the query and the rationale. After an incorrect or incomplete response, you must repeat the response and the query.

Neutral comments (hello, can you tell me..., thank you) may be made. You will be asked if you are calling long distance in some cases; no, you have a poor connection. If asked, you may volunteer the information that you are a student at the institution. No matter how tempting, please do not indicate any other information. An example that will clarify the query application process is as follows:

You: [RATIONALE], (I'm writing a letter and need to know) [QUERY], the address of the main office of Publix Markets.

Respondent: Are you a student here?

You: Yes, and I need the information for a letter. [OPTIONAL REPEAT OF THE RATIONALE]

Respondent: 2070 Tampa Highway, Lakeland, Florida 33802.

You: [INCORRECT INFORMATION, REQUIRED REPEAT OF THE RESPONSE], 2070 Tampa Highway, Lakeland...

Respondent: No, sorry, that is 2040 New Tampa Highway.

You: 2040 New Tampa Highway, Lakeland, Florida 33802 is the address of the main office of Publix Markets? [REQUIRED REPEAT OF RESPONSE AND QUERY].

[114]

Respondent: Right.

You: Great, thanks a lot!

If the library staff member indicates the source(s) that were consulted, record this information in the appropriate place on the Query Response Form. The source will generally be incomplete titles or broad types of reference books (almanacs); do not ask for further details unless specifically instructed to do so.

Use the back of the Query Response Form and attach separate sheets, if necessary, to record any additional information. Remember that this is a research study, so if doubt arises as to the pertinence of the information, write it down!

Appendix C

SURVEY OF ACADEMIC LIBRARY REFERENCE/INFORMATION
SERVICES

Instructions

This questionnaire should be completed by the librarian who super-
vises the delivery of reference/information services. Librarians responding for decentralized systems should answer for main/general
reference rather than departmental/divisional libraries. All answers
should reflect current practices or practices within the past 12 months
and not future plans.

Please return the completed questionnaire as soon as possible to:

Marcia Myers
5500 S. W. 63rd Court
Miami, Florida 33155

Developmental Guidelines

The statements in this section
have been adapted from "A
Commitment to Information
Services: Developmental
Guidelines" adopted by the
Reference and Adult Services
Division of the American Library Association in January
1976. Please indicate how
each statement reflects the
reference/information services
in your library by writing
the appropriate number (1
thru 5) in the box provided
prior to each statement using
the following key list:

1--NOT AT ALL
2--TO A LITTLE EXTENT
3--TO SOME EXTENT
4--TO A GREAT EXTENT
5--COMPLETELY

Services

[ ] 1. Reference or information services are
developed not only to
meet user needs and
to improve present
services but to antici-
pate user needs and de-
mands.

[ ] 2. A published service code
with stated objectives
is used to carry out in-
formation services and
is available to all users.

[ ] 3. The code details the
circumstances under
which services and re-
sources are offered,
the extent to which they
are provided, any limi-
tation on their provi-
sions, and to whom and
by whom such services
are provided.

[ ] 4. Reference or information services are re-
viewed at regular in-
tervals to identify
those individuals who
are and are not being
served and to deter-
mine how individuals
not utilizing such serv-
ices can be reached.

[116]

[ ] 5. Provision is made for continuous feedback from users concerning their satisfaction with services and success in locating information.

[ ] 6. A specific plan for the instruction of individuals in the use of information aids has been developed and is coordinated among all types of libraries, information centers or units of library activity.

[ ] 7. Bibliographical and other informational access guides are developed by librarians/information specialists as an active "alert" service signifying the potential of the information resource base available to users.

[ ] 8. Access to reference or information service is promoted and provided in adaptable settings, including person-to-person contact, correspondence, and/or through other communication media.

[ ] 9. There is formal cooperation among other information handling units, centers or agencies at local, regional, State and national levels to provide for the needs of all users and potential users.

[ ] 10. Referrals to other sources and agencies are a standard level of information service operation.

[ ] 11. The effectiveness of these referrals are evaluated at selected intervals to determine the effectiveness of the delivery service and the quality of the response to the user.

[ ] 12. A selection policy has been developed which addresses the needs and anticipated needs of the user and reflects the available resources to the user within an accessible area.

[ ] 13. A cooperative selection policy within a given service area has been developed.

[ ] 14. Materials are added which reflect a diversity in format, levels of information service activity (e.g., general information service, resource back-up and research capability), and known user patterns of the past.

[ ] 15. Frequently used materials are available in multiple copies in order to address user demands more quickly.

[ ] 16. All information materials are examined regularly for condition, usefulness and currency, and either retained, discarded, or replaced.

Environment

[ ] 17. Service points are as near as possible to the main focal point of

[117]

activity in the library or information center.

[ ] 18. The reference or information collection is situated so that it is near an open area where access allows for quick and effective service.

[ ] 19. Individual carrels or other provisions for quiet concentrated study are available for users of the reference or information collection.

[ ] 20. The main reference or information area is situated so that the necessary conversation between library users and librarians/information specialists is not disturbing to others.

[ ] 21. Additional service points are located so that access to librarians/information specialists is available throughout the library with communication equipment and techniques provided when appropriate.

Personnel

[ ] 22. Staffing patterns and hours open reflect directly the needs of the users.

[ ] 23. A professional librarian/information specialist is available to users during all hours the library is open.

[ ] 24. The reference or infor-

mation staff actively promotes the use of all library services. This is done by whatever means are appropriate to the institutional setting, e.g., canvassing a public library area to offer assistance.

[ ] 25. Individual librarians/information specialists have training in specific subject fields.

[ ] 26. Staff members are chosen with consideration given not only to their academic background and knowledge, but also to their ability to communicate easily with people.

[ ] 27. There has been opportunity for continuing education of the librarian/information specialist.

Evaluation

[ ] 28. User data are collected on a regular basis to determine effectiveness of information service patterns.

[ ] 29. The measurement and evaluation of reference or information services is the responsibility of one or more staff members with some skills in this field.

[ ] 30. Statistics are collected on a systematic basis for use in evaluation, policy decision, reports, and in budget preparation.

General Information

Listed below are several statements pertaining to reference/information services. Please indicate how each statement relates to services in your library by writing the appropriate number (1 thru 5) in the box provided prior to each statement using the following key list:

1--NEVER
2--RARELY
3--OCCASIONALLY
4--REGULARLY
5--ALWAYS

[ ] 31. The size (number of volumes) of the reference collection is adequate for answering reference/information questions received from users.

[ ] 32. The currency (up-to-dateness) of the reference collection is adequate for answering reference/information questions received from users.

[ ] 33. Unanswered questions are referred to a senior staff member and/or reference supervisor.

[ ] 34. Answers to fact-type questions* are verified in more than one source for accuracy and recent changes.

[ ] 35. The accuracy of the source used to answer reference information questions is the responsibility of the user.

[ ] 36. The printed source of the answer is shown to the walk-in inquirer.

[ ] 37. The source of the answer is cited for the telephone inquirer.

[ ] 38. Fact-type questions* received via telephone are answered rather than referring the inquirer to sources that contain the answer.

[ ] 39. The information for unanswered fact-type questions* is obtained from outside sources rather than referring the user to these sources.

[ ] 40. Staff meetings are held with personnel who provide reference/information services.

[ ] 41. Staff members responsible for the delivery of reference/information services are provided a written job description.

[ ] 42. Paraprofessionals answer reference questions.

[ ] 43. Paraprofessionals answer directional questions.

[ ] 44. Paraprofessionals answer fact-type questions.*

*Fact-type questions are questions that require a simple answer that may be found in one source although the library staff member may have to look in more than one source before the answer is located.

[119]

Background Information

Please enter the appropriate information in the space provided for each question.

_____ 45. Number of service points (desks) within the main reference/information area.

_____ 46. Number of F.T.E. professionals providing reference/information service.

_____ 47. Number of F.T.E. paraprofessionals providing reference/information service.

_____ 48. Number of hours per typical week library is opened to users.

_____ 49. Number of hours per typical week library offers reference/information service to users.

_____ 50. Number of directional questions answered per typical week.

_____ 51. Number of reference questions answered per typical week.

_____ 52. Number of volumes in the main/general reference collection.

_____ 53. Number of volumes shelved near the desk or telephone for answering fact-type questions.

_____ 54. Annual salary of beginning librarian in your library with master's degree in library science and no experience.

_____ 55. Number of reference/information staff who are personal members of the American Library Association.

56. What is your title?

_____

57. How many hours per week do you spend on reference/information desk duty?

_____

58. What is the highest degree you hold with a major in library science?

_____

59. What is the highest degree you hold with a major other than library science?

Degree_____
Major_____

60. In which of the following library organizations do you hold personal memberships:

[ ] ALA (American Library Association)

[ ] RASD (Reference and Adult Services Division

[ ] ACRL (Association of College and Research Libraries)

[ ] ASIS (American Society for Information Science)

[ ] SELA (Southeastern Library Association)

[ ] Other (Please specify):

Thank you for completing the questionnaire. Please use the back of this sheet to make any comments you have about the survey or your library's reference/information services.

If you would like a summary of the results, check here [ ]

Name_____

Appendix D

DISTRIBUTION OF PERFORMANCE ON DEPENDENT VARIABLES BY TYPE OF INSTITUTION AND CONTROL

Type of Control and Institution	No. of Responses	No. of Times Refusal Received	Call Back Required* No.	M.	S.D.	No. of Times Referral Made	Answered Immediately** No.	M.	S.D.	Attempted Then Call Back** No.	M.	S.D.	No. of Times Source Volunteered
All responses													
Two-Yr.													
Public	60	6	25	1.2	0.5	9	35	132	108	4	222	204	7
Private	60	7	39	1.3	0.5	17	21	160	176	5	135	153	11
Four-N.													
Public	60	5	32	1.2	0.4	14	28	223	214	7	215	152	9
Private	60	5	34	1.4	0.9	11	26	202	163	11	210	71	11
Four-G.													
Public	60	1	34	1.2	0.5	9	26	191	121	14	380	290	18
Private	60	4	37	1.1	0.4	14	23	123	113	7	228	175	18
Univ.													
Public	60	1	32	1.2	0.4	6	28	201	108	8	252	177	11
Private	60	3	26	1.0	0.2	7	34	209	174	9	296	235	23
Totals	480	32	259	1.2	0.5	87	221	181	153	65	272	202	108
Correct responses													
Two-Yr.													
Public	26	0	14	1.2	0.6	1	12	189	128	2	130	49	5
Private	25	0	23	1.2	0.5	1	2	90	21	2	442	81	4

				*					**			
Four-N. Public	22	0	12	1.3	0.5	1	10	260	214	0	0	0	1
Private	32	0	24	1.2	0.5	2	8	210	160	7	201	74	5
Four-C. Public	34	0	22	1.2	0.4	0	12	148	77	6	355	338	11
Private	31	0	23	1.1	0.3	2	3	91	73	3	300	273	11
Univ. Public	37	0	20	1.1	0.4	2	17	174	94	5	269	209	7
Private	35	0	19	1.0	0.0	0	16	214	110	5	367	285	16
Totals	242	0	157	1.2	0.4	9	35	184	128	30	292	225	60
Incorrect responses													
Two-Yr. Public	34	6	11	1.3	0.4	8	23	103	84	2	315	297	2
Private	35	7	16	1.3	0.5	16	19	167	184	3	178	42	7
Four-N. Public	38	5	20	1.1	0.3	13	18	203	217	7	215	152	8
Private	28	5	10	1.9	1.3	9	18	199	169	4	226	71	6
Four-G. Public	26	1	12	1.3	0.6	9	14	229	141	8	398	271	7
Private	29	4	14	1.1	0.5	12	15	140	129	4	175	50	7
Univ. Public	23	1	12	1.2	0.4	4	11	243	119	3	224	142	4
Private	25	3	7	1.1	0.4	7	18	203	219	4	208	143	7
Totals	238	32	102	1.3	0.6	78	136	179	167	35	256	180	48

*Number of times at least one call back was required; mean and standard deviation of the number of call backs.
**Number of times a call back was not suggested immediately; mean and standard deviation of the search time in seconds.

Appendix E

SUMMARY STATISTICS ON THE PERFORMANCE
SCORE: NUMBER OF CORRECT RESPONSES BY
LIBRARY CLASSIFICATION

Table A

STATISTICS DESCRIBING THE PERFORMANCE
SCORE: NUMBER OF CORRECT RESPONSES BY
TYPE OF CONTROL

	Libraries		Totals (N= 40)
	Public (N= 20)	Private (N= 20)	
Mode	6.00	7.00	6.00
Median	6.07	6.25	6.14
Mean	5.95	6.15	6.05
Minimum	3.00	3.00	3.00
Maximum	9.00	9.00	9.00
Range	6.00	6.00	6.00
Interquartile range	3.00	2.00	2.00
Standard deviation	1.57	1.56	1.55
Standard error	.35	.35	.24

Table B

STATISTICS DESCRIBING THE PERFORMANCE
SCORE: NUMBER OF CORRECT RESPONSES BY
TYPE OF INSTITUTION

	Libraries				
	Two-Yr. (N=10)	Four-N. (N=10)	Four-G. (N=10)	Univ. (N=10)	Totals (N=40)
Mode	4.00	6.00	. . .	. . .	6.00
Median	5.00	5.50	6.50	7.50	6.14
Mean	5.10	5.40	6.50	7.20	6.05
Minimum	4.00	3.00	5.00	3.00	3.00
Maximum	7.00	8.00	8.00	9.00	9.00
Range	3.00	5.00	3.00	6.00	6.00
Interquartile range	2.00	2.00	1.00	1.00	2.00
Standard deviation	1.10	1.51	.85	1.75	1.55
Standard error	.35	.48	.27	.55	.24

Table C

STATISTICS DESCRIBING THE PERFORMANCE SCORE:
NUMBER OF CORRECT RESPONSES BY TYPE OF INSTITUTION AND CONTROL

| | Libraries | | | | | | | | Totals (N=40) |
| | Two-Yr. | | Four-N. | | Four-G. | | Univ. | | |
	Public (N=5)	Private (N=5)	Public (N=5)	Private (N=5)	Public (N=5)	Private (N=5)	Public (N=5)	Private (N=5)	
Mode	6.00	. . .	4.00	6.00	. . .	. . .	7.00	8.00	6.00
Median	5.33	4.75	4.25	6.25	6.75	6.25	7.25	7.75	6.14
Mean	5.20	5.00	4.40	6.40	6.80	6.20	7.40	7.00	6.05
Minimum	4.00	4.00	3.00	5.00	6.00	5.00	6.00	3.00	3.00
Maximum	6.00	7.00	6.00	8.00	8.00	7.00	9.00	9.00	9.00
Range	2.00	3.00	3.00	3.00	2.00	2.00	3.00	6.00	6.00
Interquartile range	2.00	1.00	1.00	1.00	1.00	1.00	1.00	1.00	2.00
Standard deviation	1.09	1.22	1.14	1.14	.84	.84	1.14	2.34	1.55
Standard error	.49	.55	.51	.51	.37	.37	.51	1.05	.24

Appendix F

VALIDITY OF SURVEY RESPONSES

Table A

VALIDITY OF THE SURVEY RESPONSES ON THE
DEVELOPMENTAL GUIDELINES SECTIONS

Questions	Guidelines Section r_s	$\underline{p}^a$	Total Guidelines r_s	$\underline{p}^a$	Number of Correct Responses r_s	$\underline{p}^a$
1.	.67	.001	.66	.001	-.22	.091
2.	.59	.001	.48	.003	-.33	.021
3.	.59	.001	.49	.003	-.32	.025
4.	.61	.001	.62	.001	-.22	.091
5.	.31	.044	.31	.043	-.15	n.s.
6.	.63	.001	.63	.001	-.24	.074
7.	.35	.025	.34	.029	.25	.062
8.	.72	.001	.72	.001	.17	n.s.
9.	.32	.039	.32	.038	-.02	n.s.
10.	.43	.007	.22	n.s.	.22	.089
11.	.51	.001	.48	.003	.05	n.s.
12.	.48	.003	.30	.053	-.10	n.s.
13.	.54	.001	.50	.002	-.13	n.s.
14.	.66	.001	.61	.001	.04	n.s.
15.	.36	.023	.42	.009	-.29	.035
16.	.55	.001	.50	.002	-.08	n.s.
Total services	1.00^b	...	.89^c	.001	-.23^b	n.s.
17.	.69	.001	.26	.079	-.20	n.s.
18.	.70	.001	.51	.002	-.15	n.s.
19.	.79	.001	.52	.001	-.19	n.s.
20.	.84	.001	.56	.001	-.09	n.s.
21.	.45	.003	.33	.035	.01	n.s.
Total environment	1.00^d	...	.61^c	.001	-.14^d	n.s.
22.	.54	.001	.63	.001	.09	n.s.
23.	.69	.001	.45	.005	.30	.032
24.	.38	.010	.44	.007	-.09	n.s.
25.	.54	.001	.40	.012	.09	n.s.
26.	.52	.001	.45	.005	-.03	n.s.
27.	.53	.001	.34	.030	.10	n.s.
Total personnel	1.00^d	...	.68^c	.001	.18^d	n.s.
28.	.85	.001	.64	.001	-.11	n.s.
29.	.94	.001	.77	.001	-.18	n.s.
30.	.85	.001	.63	.001	-.00	n.s.
Total evaluation	1.00^a	...	.79^c	.001	-.11^e	n.s.
Total guidelines	...	...	1.00	...	-.20^c	n.s.

^{a}n.s. means p > .10; since responses with missing values were
excluded pairwise from the calculations, only the total N is indicated
as follows: b = 32, c = 31, d = 37, e = 38.

Table B

VALIDITY OF THE SURVEY RESPONSES ON THE
GENERAL INFORMATION SECTION

Questions	General Information Section		Number of Correct Responses	
	r_s	p^a	r_s	p^a
31.	.26	.069	- .09	n. s.
32.	.50	.001	- .04	n. s.
33.	.60	.001	.01	n. s.
34.	.26	.067	- .20	n. s.
35. b	.20	n. s.	.30	n. s.
36.	.30	.040	- .06	n. s.
37.	.22	n. s.	- .11	n. s.
38.	.42	.007	.01	n. s.
39.	.28	.056	- .13	n. s.
40.	.39	.011	.09	n. s.
41.	.34	.023	.05	n. s.
42. b	.61	.001	.23	.080
43. b	.53	.001	.17	n. s.
44. b	.60	.001	.21	.099
Total questions 31 through 44	1.00^a	. . .	$.12^a$	n. s.

[a]n. s. means $p > .10$; responses with missing values were excluded pairwise from the calculations, the total N was 34.
[b]Survey responses were reversed for scoring.

Table C

VALIDITY OF THE SURVEY RESPONSES ON THE
BACKGROUND INFORMATION SECTION

Questions	Background Statistics Section		Number of Correct Responses	
	r_s	p^a	r_s	p^a
45.	.20	n. s.	.15	n. s.
46.	.44	.042	.31	.027
47.	.06	n. s.	-.25	.068
48.	.62	.005	.62	.001
49.	.41	.058	.54	.001
50.	.79	.001	.48	.003
51.	.70	.001	.32	.037
52.	.62	.007	.67	.001
53.	.17	n. s.	.27	.048
54.	-.22	n. s.	.06	n. s.
55.	.47	.034	.40	.007
Total questions 45 through 55	1.00[a]	. . .	.77[a]	.001

[a]n. s. means $p > .10$; responses with missing values were
excluded pairwise from the calculations; the total N was 16.

[129]

Appendix G

RAW AND RANK ORDER DATA ON REFERENCE VOLUMES HELD,
HOURS OF SERVICE PER WEEK, AND NUMBER OF CORRECT RESPONSES BY LIBRARY

Volumes, Reference	Rank Vols. Reference	Hours Ref. Per Week	Rank Hrs./Wk.	No. of Correct Responses	Library No.	Type of Institution	Type of Control
350	1	67.0	10	5	6	Two-Yr.	Private
1,000	2	65.0	8	6	2	Two-Yr.	Public
1,200	3	80.0	19	6	24	Four-G.	Public
2,000	4	70.0	11	4	7	Two-Yr.	Private
2,000	4	66.2	9	4	1	Two-Yr.	Public
2,267	6	61.4	6	4	4	Two-Yr.	Public
2,350	7	64.5	7	6	3	Two-Yr.	Public
2,467	8	40.0	2	6	5	Two-Yr.	Public
2,750	9	74.0	15	3	11	Four-N.	Public
3,600	10	40.0	2	6	12	Four-N.	Public
3,800	11	35.0	1	4	15	Four-N.	Public
5,000	12	73.0	14	6	20	Four-N.	Private

6,500	13	60.0	5	4	13	Four-N.	Public
6,600	14	45.0	4	5	18	Four-N.	Private
7,000	15	89.0	23	8	21	Four-G.	Public
8,000	16	96.0	24	7	35	Univ.	Public
9,324	17	70.0	11	6	17	Four-N.	Private
17,682	18	87.0	22	6	33	Univ.	Public
20,000	19	80.0	17	8	19	Four-N.	Private
20,000	19	80.0	17	7	23	Four-G.	Public
20,000	19	82.0	20	6	25	Four-G.	Public
20,000	19	83.5	21	8	36	Univ.	Private
20,000	19	77.0	16	7	37	Univ.	Private
23,534	24	71.0	13	8	34	Univ.	Public
26,500	25	100.0	25	9	31	Univ.	Public

Appendix H

STATISTICS DESCRIBING REFERENCE VOLUMES HELD BY TYPE OF INSTITUTION

	Libraries				Totals (N=25)
	Two-Yr. (N=7)	Four-N. (N=8)	Four-G. (N=4)	Univ. (N=6)	
Mode	2,000	. . .	20,000	20,000	20,000
Median	2,021	5,050	9,900	20,000	6,500
Mean	1,776	7,197	12,050	19,286	9,357
Minimum	350	2,750	1,200	8,000	350
Maximum	2,467	20,000	20,000	26,500	26,500
Range	2,117	17,250	18,800	18,500	26,150
Interquartile range	1,350	3,000	18,800	5,852	17,650
Standard deviation	794	5,585	9,480	6,341	8,546
Standard error	300	1,975	4,740	2,589	1,709

Appendix I

STATISTICS DESCRIBING HOURS OF REFERENCE SERVICE PER WEEK
BY TYPE OF INSTITUTION

| | Libraries | | | | |
	Two-Yr. (N=7)	Four-N. (N=8)	Four-G. (N=4)	Univ. (N=6)	Totals (N=25)
Mode	. . .	. . .	80.0	. . .	80.0
Median	65.0	60.5	81.0	85.2	71.0
Mean	62.0	59.6	82.7	85.7	70.3
Minimum	40.0	35.0	80.0	71.0	35.0
Maximum	70.0	80.0	89.0	100.0	100.0
Range	30.0	45.0	9.0	29.0	65.0
Interquartile range	5.6	33.0	9.0	19.0	15.5
Standard deviation	10.0	17.4	4.3	11.0	16.9
Standard error	3.8	6.1	2.1	4.5	3.4

[133]

NOTES

Introduction

1. American Library Association, Reference and Adult Services Division, Standards Committee, "A Commitment to Information Services: Developmental Guidelines," RQ 15 (Summer 1976): 327-29; hereafter referred to as "Developmental Guidelines."

2. Samuel Rothstein, "The Measurement and Evaluation of Reference Service," Library Trends 12 (January 1964): 459.

3. Marcia J. Myers, "The Effectiveness of Telephone Reference/Information Services in Academic Libraries in the Southeast," (Ph.D. dissertation, Florida State University, 1979); "The Guidelines and Performance in Academic Libraries," in Is Reference Progressing? A Look at the Guidelines for Information Service Three Years Later, Reference and Adult Services Division (Chicago: American Library Association, 1979), Conference Cassette 351 and 352; "The Accuracy of Telephone Reference Services in the Southeast: A Case for Quantitative Standards," in Library Effectiveness: A State of the Art, Library Administration and Management Association (Chicago: American Library Association, 1980), pp. 219-33.

Chapter 1

1. F. W. Lancaster, The Measurement and Evaluation of Library Services (Washington, D.C.: Information Resources Press, 1977), p. 74.

2. Terry L. Weech, "Evaluation of Adult Reference Service," Library Trends 22 (January 1974): 331.

3. Terence Crowley and Thomas Childers, Information Service in Public Libraries: Two Studies (Metuchen, N.J.: Scarecrow, 1971).

4. Lowell A. Martin, "User Studies and Library Planning," Library Trends 24 (January 1976): 485.

5. Samuel Rothstein, The Development of Reference Services Through Academic Traditions, Public Library Practice, and Special Librarianship (Chicago: Association of College and Reference Libraries, 1955).

6. Margaret Hutchins, Introduction to Reference Work (Chicago: American Library Association, 1944), pp. 201-04.

7. William A. Katz, Introduction to Reference Work, Vol. 2: Reference Services and Reference Processes, 2d ed. (New York: McGraw-Hill, 1974), p. 59.

8. Weech, pp. 315-35; Nice M. de Figueiredo, "A Conceptual Methodology for Error Prevention in Reference Work" (Ph.D. dissertation, Florida State University, 1975); Marjorie E. Murfin and Lubomyr R. Wynar, Reference Service: An Annotated Bibliographic Guide (Littleton, Colo.: Libraries Unlimited, 1977); Lancaster.

9. Crowley and Childers, pp. 1-84.

10. Ibid., pp. 73-204.

11. Peat, Marwick, Mitchell and Company, California Public Library Systems: A Comprehensive Review with Guidelines for the Next Decade (Los Angeles: Peat, Marwick, Mitchell and Company, 1975).

12. Weech, p. 331.

13. R. Sergean, Letter to the Editor, Library Quarterly 43 (January 1973): 64-65; Thomas Childers, "The Author Responds," Library Quarterly 43 (January 1973): 65.

14. Ronald Rowe Powell, "An Investigation of the Relationship Between Reference Collection Size and Other Refer-

ence Service Factors and Success in Answering Reference Questions" (Ph. D. dissertation, University of Illinois, 1976).

15. Robert R. Haro, review of Information Service in Public Libraries: Two Studies, by Terence Crowley and Thomas Childers, in College and Research Libraries 33 (September 1972): 411.

16. Geraldine B. King and Rachel Berry, Evaluation of the University of Minnesota Libraries Reference Department Telephone Information Service: Pilot Study (Minneapolis: University of Minnesota Library School, 1973; ERIC Document Reproduction Service, ED 077 517).

17. "'Unobtrusive Testing' Used in Ohio Survey," News from the State Library of Ohio 133 (October 24, 1972): 88-89.

18. Ruth W. White, ed., A Study of Reference Services and Reference Users in the Metropolitan Atlanta Area (Athens: Department of Library Education, Georgia University, 1971; ERIC Document Reproduction Service, ED 058 912).

19. Billy Rayford Wilkinson, "Reference Services for Undergraduate Students: Four Case Studies" (D. L. S. dissertation, Columbia University, 1971); Abram Venable Lawson, "Reference Service in University Libraries, Two Case Studies" (D. L. S. dissertation, Columbia University, 1971).

20. Cynthia B. Duncan, "An Analysis of Tasks Performed by Reference Personnel in College and in University Libraries in Indiana" (Ph. D. dissertation, Indiana University, 1974).

Chapter 2

1. National Center for Education Statistics, Library Statistics of Colleges and Universities, Fall, 1975, Institutional Data (Washington, D. C.: U. S. Government Printing Office, 1977); hereafter referred to as Library Statistics of Colleges and Universities.

2. Weech, p. 332.

3. Crowley and Childers, p. 125.

4. Leslie Kish, Survey Sampling (New York: Wiley, 1965), p. 103.

5. Gerald Jahoda, The Process of Answering Reference Questions: A Test of a Descriptive Model (Tallahassee: Florida State University School of Library Science, 1977; ERIC Document Reproduction Service, ED 136 769).

6. Joseph E. Hill and August Kerber, Models, Methods and Analytical Procedures in Education Research (Detroit: Wayne State University Press, 1967), p. 69.

7. Hubert M. Blalock, Jr., Social Statistics, 2nd ed. (New York: McGraw-Hill, 1972), p. 271.

8. For example, see Sidney Siegel, Nonparametric Statistics for the Behavioral Sciences (New York: McGraw-Hill, 1956).

9. Norman H. Nie and others, SPSS: Statistical Package for the Social Sciences, 2nd ed. (New York: McGraw-Hill, 1975).

Chapter 3

1. Eugene J. Webb and others, Unobtrusive Measures: Nonreactive Research in the Social Sciences (Chicago: Rand McNally, 1966), pp. 169-70; Crowley and Childers, p. 120.

2. William J. Reichman, Use and Abuse of Statistics (New York: Oxford University Press, 1962), p. 246.

3. Eugene P. Sheehy, comp., Guide to Reference Books, 9th ed. (Chicago: American Library Association, 1976).

4. The Alexandria Quartet is recommended in Books for College Libraries (Chicago: American Library Association, 1967), II: 306, and in James W. Pirie, comp., Books for Junior College Libraries (Chicago: American Library Association, 1969), p. 226.

5. American Library Association, The ALA Yearbook; A Review of Library Events, 1975 (Chicago: The Association, 1976), p. 83.

6. Herbert Goldhor, A Plan for the Development of Public Library Service in the Minneapolis-St. Paul Metropolitan Area (Minneapolis: Metropolitan Library Service Agency, January 1967), p. 28.

7. Crowley and Childers, p. 143.

8. Sheehy, p. 302.

9. Crowley and Childers, p. 65.

10. King and Bryant, pp. 286-88.

11. For formulas on the weighted mean and its variance, see Kish, pp. 77-79; a similar end-product can be obtained using the SPSS weighting process as detailed in Nie, pp. 129-31.

Chapter 5

1. Association of College and Research Libraries, "Standards for College Libraries," College and Research Libraries News 36 (October 1975): 279.

2. Southern Association of Colleges and Schools, Standards of the College Delegate Assembly (Atlanta: The Association, December 1, 1971), p. 17.

Chapter 6

1. Powell, pp. 91-93.

BIBLIOGRAPHY

American Library Association. Reference and Adult Services Division. Standards Committee. "A Commitment to Information Services: Developmental Guidelines." RQ 15 (Summer 1976): 327-29.

Crowley, Terence, and Thomas Childers. Information Service in Public Libraries: Two Studies. Metuchen, N.J.: Scarecrow, 1971.

Duncan, Cynthia B. "An Analysis of Tasks Performed by Reference Personnel in College and in University Libraries in Indiana." Ph.D. dissertation, Indiana, 1974.

Figueiredo, Nice M. de. "A Conceptual Methodology for Error Prevention in Reference Work." Ph.D. dissertation, Florida State University, 1975.

Jahoda, Gerald, and associates. The Reference Process: Modules for Instruction. Tallahassee: School of Library Science, Florida State University, January 1976.

King, Donald W., and Edward C. Bryant. The Evaluation of Information Services and Products. Washington, D.C.: Information Resources Press, 1971.

King, Geraldine B., and Rachel Berry. Evaluation of the University of Minnesota Libraries Reference Department Telephone Information Service: Pilot Study. Minneapolis: University of Minnesota, Library School, 1973. ERIC Document Reproduction Service, ED 077 517.

Lancaster, F. W. The Measurement and Evaluation of Library Services. Washington, D.C.: Information Resources Press, 1977.

Lawson, Abram Venable. "Reference Service in University Libraries: Two Case Studies." D. L. S. dissertation, Columbia University, 1971.

National Center for Education Statistics. Library Statistics of Colleges and Universities, Fall 1975, Institutional Data. Washington, D. C.: U. S. Government Printing Office, 1977.

Nie, Norman H., and others. SPSS: Statistical Package for the Social Sciences. 2nd ed. New York: McGraw-Hill, 1975.

Peat, Marwick, Mitchell and Company. California Public Library Systems: A Comprehensive Review with Guidelines for the Next Decade. Los Angeles: Peat, Marwick, Mitchell and Company, 1975. ERIC Document Reproduction Service, ED 105 906.

Powell, Ronald R. "An Investigation of the Relationship Between Reference Collection Size and Other Reference Service Factors and Success in Answering Reference Questions." Ph. D. dissertation, University of Illinois, 1976.

Rothstein, Samuel. "The Measurement and Evaluation of Reference Service." Library Trends 12 (January 1964): 456-72.

Schiller, Anita R. "Reference Service: Instruction or Information." Library Quarterly 35 (January 1965): 52-60.

Sheehy, Eugene P., comp. Guide to Reference Books. 9th ed. Chicago: American Library Association, 1976.

Siegel, Sidney. Nonparametric Statistics for the Behavioral Sciences. New York: McGraw-Hill, 1956.

"'Unobtrusive Testing' Used in Ohio Survey." News from the State Library of Ohio. 133 (October 24, 1972): 88-89.

Weech, Terry L. "Evaluation of Adult Reference Service." Library Trends 22 (January 1974): 315-35.

White, Ruth W., ed. A Study of Reference Services and Reference Users in the Metropolitan Atlanta Area. Athens: Department of Library Education, Georgia University, 1971. ERIC Document Reproduction Service, ED 058 912.

Wilkinson, Billy R. "Reference Services for Undergraduate Students: Four Case Studies." D.L.S. dissertation, Columbia University, 1971.

Part II:

TELEPHONE REFERENCE/INFORMATION
SERVICES IN SELECTED NORTHEASTERN
COLLEGE LIBRARIES

by
Jassim M. Jirjees

CONTENTS: PART II

Acknowledgments 146

1. INTRODUCTION TO THE STUDY 148
2. REVIEW OF THE LITERATURE 157
3. METHODOLOGY 169
4. FINDINGS: UNOBTRUSIVE MEASURES
   AND THE CASE STUDY 184
5. FINDINGS: INDEPENDENT AND
   DEPENDENT VARIABLES 196
6. FINDINGS: THE QUESTIONS 209
7. SUMMARY, CONCLUSIONS, AND
   COMMENTS 234

Appendices

A. Query response form 244
B. Instructions for test reference questions 246
C. Questionnaire for reference staff members 247
D. Survey of academic library reference/
   information services 249
E. Childers's scale of correctness (Scale A)
   and its code 253
F. Statistics describing the five minor
   dependent variables 254
G. Correct answers, by library 255
H. Correct answers, by question 256

Notes 257
Bibliography 263

[144]

LIST OF TABLES AND FIGURES

Tables

1. Categories of Questions   174

2. Correlations Between the Independent Variables and the Major Dependent Variable   201

3. Correlations Between the Three Categories and the Major Dependent Variable   202

4. Correlation Matrix: The Independent Variables   204

5. Correlation Matrix: Independent and Minor Dependent Variables   207

6. Frequency and Percentage Distribution of Response Performance   229

7. Frequency and Percentage Distribution of Number of Calls Made to a Library   230

8. Sources Volunteered   231

9. Chi-Square Test of Performance by Categories of Questions   232

Figures

1. Conceptual Overview of Problem Area   149

2. Reference Problem Investigated in This Study   150

[145]

ACKNOWLEDGMENTS

Sincere thanks are extended to my committee members, Dr. Thomas Childers, Dr. Ernest De Prospo, Dr. Esther Dyer, Dr. Bernard Goldstein, and Dr. Douglas Jones for all they contributed to my research. Special thanks go to Dr. Ralph Blasingame, the Chairperson of the Committee, whose considerable assistance and advice have always been available. I would like also to thank Dr. Marcia J. Myers, who shared her experience and information about her own work in the field of reference services. The advice of Dr. Jeffrey Smith of the Graduate School of Education, is deeply appreciated. Thanks are also due to Dr. Terence Crowley, who made many helpful comments on the reference performance test questions. I am greatly indebted to Mary Ross for typing my rough drafts and Mary Lou Thompson for typing the final manuscript.

Many colleagues at the Graduate School of Library and Information Services of Rutgers University contributed directly and indirectly to my efforts. I particularly wish to thank Dr. David Carr, Virgil Blake, Stephen Force, Betty Turock, and Joseph Ravelli.

My acknowledgments could not be complete without mention of the twenty-two reference librarians at Rutgers who served as an expert panel in reviewing and judging the usability of the reference performance test questions. Special mention is hereby given to the thirty-five anonymous proxies whose participation in the reference performance test made this study possible.

This study could not have been undertaken without the scholarship awarded by the Iraqi Ministry of Higher Education and Scientific Research.

[146]

Special gratitude goes to my wife, Basila A. Lilu, who had to stand my bad temper during the process of writing this work.

Finally, I wish to dedicate this work to Basil, Nawfal, and Feras, my children, and a generation in the making.

1.
INTRODUCTION TO THE STUDY

The primary objective of this study was to apply the technique of unobtrusive measurement, developed by Crowley and Childers,[1] for the evaluation of accuracy of response to factual inquiries coming to reference departments of public libraries, in academic libraries. The work reported here was based on a doctoral dissertation. Readers who are interested in a more detailed treatment should consult the original work.[2]

An overview of the general problem area of this study is illustrated in Figure 1. It includes the preconditions of reference service and the output of that service and spectrum for the measurement of accuracy of response to requests for factual inquiries via telephone. It is known that the reference service in any library constitutes a variety of activities. The variety and diversity of reference service make it difficult for any researcher to study all the possible dimensions of reference services as a whole. This investigation studies a facet of reference/information service: the accuracy of response to factual inquiries coming to reference departments in academic libraries via telephone.

A survey of the previous studies done in the area of a library reference service revealed that a large number of variables affect the quality of reference service. The problem investigated in this study has been narrowed to those variables that research has shown to be most discriminating in outlining the quality of reference service. The definite problem studied here is displayed in Figure 2.

Specifically, the research will investigate the relation-

Figure 1.

CONCEPTUAL OVERVIEW OF PROBLEM AREA

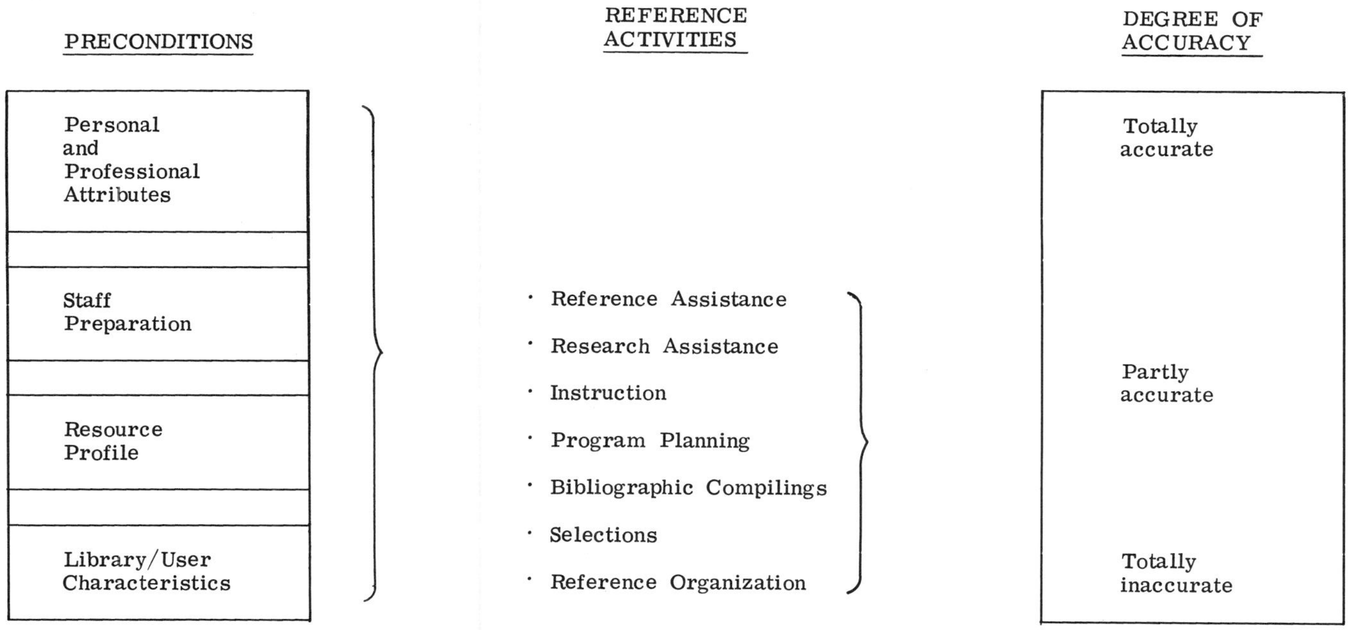

PRECONDITIONS

- Personal and Professional Attributes

- Staff Preparation

- Resource Profile

- Library/User Characteristics

REFERENCE ACTIVITIES

· Reference Assistance

· Research Assistance

· Instruction

· Program Planning

· Bibliographic Compilings

· Selections

· Reference Organization

DEGREE OF ACCURACY

Totally accurate

Partly accurate

Totally inaccurate

Figure 2.

REFERENCE PROBLEM INVESTIGATED IN THIS STUDY

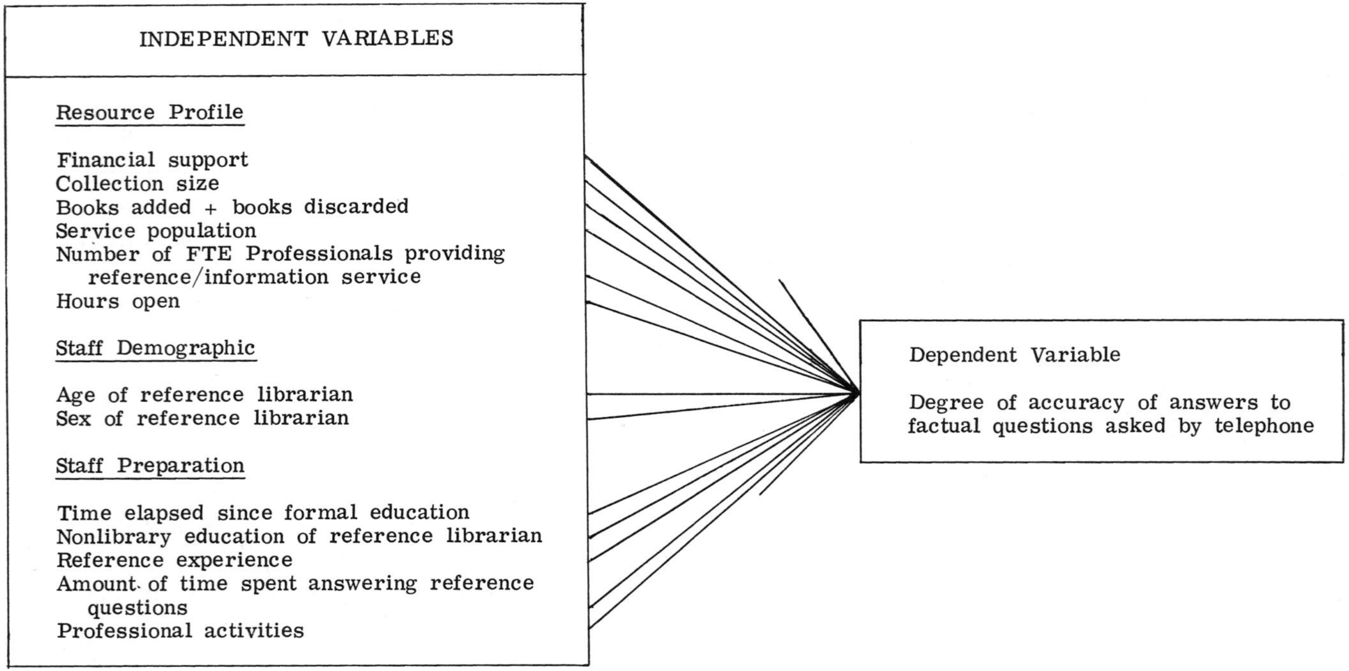

INDEPENDENT VARIABLES

Resource Profile

Financial support
Collection size
Books added + books discarded
Service population
Number of FTE Professionals providing
  reference/information service
Hours open

Staff Demographic

Age of reference librarian
Sex of reference librarian

Staff Preparation

Time elapsed since formal education
Nonlibrary education of reference librarian
Reference experience
Amount of time spent answering reference
  questions
Professional activities

Dependent Variable

Degree of accuracy of answers to
factual questions asked by telephone

ships between reference performance in the libraries of certain four-year state colleges that have graduate programs, as measured by the success in answering fact-type queries coming by telephone, and quantifiable variables (e.g., collection size, hours open) that have already been identified in the scholarly literature of library and information science as affecting the quality of reference/information service.

Research Hypothesis

Based in large part on the survey of related literature and research, the following research hypothesis was developed:

There is a positive correlation between reference performance in academic libraries (dependent variable) and each of the following independent variables: (1) financial support, (2) collection size, (3) books added + books discarded, (4) service population, (5) number of FTE professionals providing reference/information services, (6) hours open, (7) age of reference librarian, (8) sex of reference librarian, (9) time elapsed since formal education, (10) nonlibrary education of reference librarian, (11) reference experience, (12) amount of time spent answering reference/information questions, and (13) professional activities.

Assumptions

The four assumptions underlying the hypotheses are:

1. Some of the independent variables will have stronger correlation than others in terms of quality of reference service.

2. Other things being equal, there should be no difference in performance of reference service by telephone among the sample libraries.

3. When a reference librarian receives a telephone question, he or she has to give an answer and not direction, as is often the case with a question posed in person.

4. The unobtrusive technique can be used to measure

the quality of the reference/information telephone
service that an academic library of the type under
investigation provides for its clientele and that
such study will approximate at least a part of the
real picture.

Importance of the Study

The significance of the present research lies in the
fact that it ought to help in giving the profession greater insight into its own group activities. Similar to other studies
done in the area of evaluation, the present investigation will
help to identify strengths and weaknesses of one aspect of
reference/information services in the sample libraries. As
a result of having such information, it is believed that reference librarians can and will set more realistic goals for
themselves.

Another possible outcome of the study will be its con-
tribution in the pre-service and in-service education of reference librarians. The library literature has always suggested
that it is not possible for library schools to produce completely prepared reference librarians. This improvement in
one's effectiveness as a reference librarian does not necessarily come from experience alone. There has always been
a need to help reference librarians become more proficient
on the job. Workshops, conferences, and various in-service
training programs are used to meet this need in part. This
study should identify some of the parameters of the problems
and guide these various in-service programs to meet the
identified needs of reference librarians. As for the pre-
service education, one can cite Childers, who stated that
"research in this area holds potential implications for teaching reference work in library schools."[3]

The theory that quality is highly related to quantity
has been debated in the library literature for quite a number
of years. It has been suggested that "the quality of a library's service is strongly related to the quantifiable resources of that same library."[4] This study is another attempt to determine whether this perception has any empirical basis. Moreover, many researchers in the field have
pointed out that an investigation for the evaluation of refer-
ence/information service in academic libraries using unobtrusive measures is needed. The present study meets this
need by investigating whether the findings of Crowley and

Childers are limited to public libraries or are appropriate for academic libraries as well.

Definitions of Terms

For the purpose of this study the following definitions apply:

Reference service. Personal assistance provided to users in pursuit of information. The character and extent of such services will vary. This service may range from answering an apparently simple query to supplying information based on a bibliographical search combining the library/ information specialist's competence in information handling techniques with competence in the subject of inquiry. The feature is to provide an end-product in terms of information sought by the user.

Financial support. Number of dollars devoted to the total library operating expenditures for the academic year 1979-1980.

Collection size. Number of volumes as reported in Library Statistics of Colleges and Universities. [5]

Service population. Number of FTE students and faculty of the institution.

Nonlibrary education. Degrees in other subject areas.

Reference experience. Number of years in reference service.

Fact-type questions. Reference questions that usually do not require negotiation and can be satisfied by predetermined short answers.

Professional activity. This activity will be measured in number of memberships in professional library and information science organizations, offices held in these organizations, number of meetings, workshops attended, and speeches and papers presented there.

Professional organizations. Dues-paying members, at least regional in membership.

Professional meetings attended. Any meeting of a professional organization attended by the reference librarian; professional organizations had to have regional (at least) membership makeup.

Papers presented or talks given. Talks, papers, panel discussions, or other planned participation relating to the dissemination of information at a professional meeting.

Limitations of the Study

There are certain limitations of this study that should be noted. The most important ones are listed below:

1. The study was limited to only five four-year state colleges with graduate programs in the northeastern states. With this limitation and the nature of the research methods used, it would not be possible to generate theories that would be applicable to reference service in other academic libraries.

2. Only fact-type questions were used in this study.

3. This study did not examine the effectiveness of the whole reference/information service but was concerned with only one aspect of that service: the accuracy of responses to factual inquiries posed by telephone.

4. The study was limited to the 1979 spring and 1980 fall semesters.

Ethical Issues

In the literature, there is no consensus among social scientists concerning the ethical issues involved in using unobtrusive measures as a data gathering technique. The most controversial issue is the obligations of researchers to those observed. Ethical absolutism and ethical relativism represent two extreme positions concerning the ethics of social research. While only a small number of researchers have attached themselves to either of these two extremes, the volume of their exhortation has soured the research climate for others by ignoring the ethical maxim in social and behavioral research, i.e., the potential scientific benefits outweigh any possible risks to subjects.[6]

To the ethical absolutists, disguised observer roles and many unobtrusive techniques are unethical because permission for their use has not been obtained from those studied. That was exactly the point reflected in Sergean's criticism of Childers's use of the unobtrusive technique in his study of telephone information service in public libraries.[7] To accept this position means that every investigator must have permission from his or her subjects. This approach, as Denzin puts it, has the potential of making every discipline "a profession that studies only volunteer subjects."[8]

On the other hand, there are the ethical relativists, who believe that researchers have the right to make observations on anyone in any setting to the extent that they do so for scientific purposes, and do not harm the subjects. According to this position, the burden of ethical decision is placed on the personal-scientific conscience of the investigator.

The present researcher subscribes to the generally accepted scientific-objectives versus subject-risks position that supports neither the ethical absolutism nor the ethical relativism. In this position, recognition is given to the fact that a researcher's ethical obligation must match the study risks. One might cite Smith, who indicates that in research involving human subjects "the researcher must be prepared to ask: Are the scientific objectives of the study proportionate to the risks to the study subjects?"[9]

It is the belief of the present investigator that the study provided useful information and the chances of risks to subjects were minimal. It is true that the nature of the research was disguised; however, the study did not manipulate the behavior of its subjects (reference staff members) in any way. Thus, known or foreseeable risks to subjects were outweighed by the probable benefits that might accrue to them and/or humanity by their project participation. During the test period, all reference librarians had to do was to carry on with their job: answering reference questions. This was not an unusual act on their part, and the study did not change their behavior.

In a draft entitled "Ethics of Service," prepared by RASD's Standards Committee, it is stated that "information provided the user in response to an inquiry must be the most accurate possible."[10] This study aimed at developing measures of testing that standard. This could not be reasonably done solely using volunteers, and it could not be done under circumstances where the research was controlled by the subjects.

2.
REVIEW OF THE LITERATURE

The evaluation of library reference/information services in general, and reference questions and their answers in particular, has received considerable attention in the literature over a comparatively long period of time. Furthermore, as Rothstein pointed out, "the literature of this subject has itself spawned a fair-sized literature of review."[1] A thorough study of this literature reveals that the following trends are the most common characteristics of the measurement and evaluation studies identified by the scholars of reference services.

First, most studies are concerned with measurement rather than evaluation of reference services. Second, much of the literature has focused on discussing the lack of evaluation or the shortcomings of the evaluation that has taken place. Third, most of the measures and evaluations to date consist of simple counts (number of people served, number of inquiries, number of answers or nonanswers), the types of questions (directional, fact, research, reader's advisory), or the time or the number of sources required to answer the question. Fourth, the research necessary to form a basis for measurement and evaluation has been attempted only spasmodically, and then touching on only one aspect of the total program. Finally, in terms of commitment of total staff time, reference service is not an important element in library operations.

In 1942, Elizabeth O. Stone found the following methods of measuring and evaluating reference services:

(1) by classifying questions as to types; (2) time

spent on work; (3) analysis of a given number of
questions; (4) by considering the value of the information; (5) by rating the qualities or traits de-
sirable in the reference worker; (6) by analyzing
each different kind of work done by reference staff,
and time devoted to each; (7) time readers spend
in the library; (8) number of questions asked; (9) by
compiling a list of questions for which satisfactory
answers were not found; and (10) by a spot survey.[2]

The above list clearly indicates that all the approaches
Stone could find centered on what the reference librarian did,
and that "none of these [methods] adequately measure the
value of reference service." Stone emphasized the need for
a careful study and a formulation of a detailed plan that would
enable the reference service to be evaluated.

Rothstein's 1964 review of the literature of reference
service, although it was done twenty-two years after that of
Stone, did not produce a new approach in the study of that
service. Most of the evaluation had been statistical or quantitative measurement rather than evaluative. Rothstein also
reported that most librarians claim high success rates in the
answering of reference questions, varying from 88 percent to
99.7 percent.[3]

In 1974, T. L. Weech in an outstanding review of the
literature on the evaluation of adult reference services, cited
earlier, indicated that the types of measurement referred to
by Rothstein were still popular and that measurement was
still the keynote rather than evaluation. He reported that
contrary to the high level of user satisfaction and the high
degree of success reported by librarians in earlier studies,
the results of studies using test questions and unobtrusive
measures indicated that most libraries that had been evaluated up to 1974 were able to answer correctly just slightly
more than half of the questions posed.[4]

In his 1977 book on the measurement and evaluation of
library services, Lancaster reported that most evaluation of
the effectiveness of reference services was still statistical,
that the majority of data collection was being carried out in
the area of macroevaluation, and that unobtrusive observation
of reference performance was a significant trend in reference
services evaluation.[5]

The rest of this section will be devoted to a discussion

of some studies that have used reference questions and their answers as a means of evaluation of reference performance. Such studies usually utilize one of two approaches: obtrusive or unobtrusive measurement to determine the ability of reference librarians in providing answers to the patrons' questions. The major criticism against the obtrusive approach (not to hold its counterapproach as being totally perfect) is that the testing situation might contaminate the results. It is reasonable to expect that a reference librarian would act differently when he or she knows that a test situation is in existence. Among representative studies that used this approach are those done by Bunge, Powell, Goldhor, Little, and the two studies of the New York State Public Library Systems.[6] These studies have been adequately reviewed elsewhere[7] and will not be treated here.

As for the unobtrusive measurement, in 1967 Terence Crowley introduced the technique to the testing of the effectiveness of reference/information services in public libraries. Crowley's pioneering study together with that of Childers represent the most important works on unobtrusive evaluation to date.

The purpose of Crowley's study[8] was to develop a methodology for comparing the information services available to adult patrons of two sample groups of public libraries, in order to test the hypotheses that libraries with a high expenditure and high per capita support would answer a larger proportion of information questions than would libraries with low expenditures and low per capita support.

The study was conducted among medium-sized libraries open a minimum of sixty hours per week. Out of forty candidate libraries in New Jersey, six high-expenditure and six low-expenditure libraries were selected for evaluation. Anonymous proxies asked each of the "high" and "low" libraries a total of ten questions at a variety of times; half of the questions required some knowledge of current affairs for correct answering and the remainder embodied various elements calling for particular search strategies. All but one of the questions were posed by telephone.

Although the "high" libraries did answer a higher proportion of questions (thirty-six vs. sixty) than the "low" libraries (twenty-nine vs. sixty), no statistically significant differences between the two types of libraries could be found. The overall score for the entire group of libraries, 65 vs. 120, or 54.2 percent, was not especially impressive.

Lancaster, in his book The Measurement and Evaluation of Library Services, cited above, considered Crowley's study as a "valuable" one for the following reasons:

> (a) he produced for the first time a reasonable, unobtrusive approach to testing the quality of reference work, and (b) he cast serious doubts on the quality of reference work conducted in certain public libraries. Moreover, he clearly demonstrated that it is not enough to judge reference work by the number of questions that are answered; the proportion of questions answered correctly must be determined.[9]

The second important study of reference service was conducted by Thomas Childers and was published with Crowley's study in 1971. This study was carried on in an effort to measure the quality of telephone information service in public libraries.

Twenty-six questions of simple factual type were telephoned to the stratified sample of twenty-five public libraries in New Jersey. Responses were judged for correctness on each of five different scales, including two correct/not correct dichotomies and an attempt/no-attempt dichotomy. Analysis of variance and stepwise linear regression analysis were used to measure the relationships.

The findings of this study showed that approximately 64 percent of the attempted answers were correct. When no-attempt responses were scored zero, the percentage of correct answers dropped to approximately fifty-five. Comparison of the correlations between these scales indicated that there was no relationship between attempting to find an answer and success in responding correctly.

This study also showed that there was a significant variation in the correctness of response, when the libraries were stratified according to total expenditures. That is, the libraries in the lowest of the four categories of total expenditures responded accurately to significantly fewer questions than did the libraries in the highest category. However, the differences, while statistically significant, were not great.

At this point, it may be worthwhile to compare Crowley's and Childers's studies. Both had at least three things in common. First, they examined unobtrusively the accuracy of response by reference staff in public libraries. Second, the two studies used the contrived-observation technique. That is, the questions did not arise spontaneously from the environment but were compiled and applied by the investigators. Third, their studies, as far as the proportion of questions answered correctly by the reference librarians was concerned, were amazingly similar and their findings showed that just under 55 percent of the responses were correct.

However, there were many differences:

1. The number of the sample libraries in Childers's study was larger than that of Crowley's.

2. While Childers asked twenty-six questions, Crowley asked only eight, one of which was administered three times to determine consistency in library responses.

3. Whereas Crowley's test emphasized questions on current events, Childers's included a wider range of questions.

4. Childers examined forty-seven independent variables while Crowley considered one single independent variable: the total expenditures.

5. Unlike Crowley, who judged a response to be either correct or incorrect, Childers developed five scales of "correctness," where the response was judged on continuum from right to wrong.

Both Crowley and Childers have continued to apply the unobtrusive techniques systematically in a number of states to a variety of public libraries from very small to medium sized. In the 1969 study of the Chicago Public Library, [10] Lowell Martin, with the assistance of Crowley, used a panel of "anonymous shoppers" to determine actual performance by librarians when users seek help. The "shoppers" were given a set of questions that were designed to test the accuracy of information provided, skill of staff in reference searching, awareness of current trends and publications, background of book knowledge, and disposition of staff to follow through on inquiries.

It is not clear from the study how the responses were judged and how many queries were involved. Neither the ex-

act questions asked nor the accuracy of the answers were included. What we find in the study are examples of few questions on which performance was clearly deficient. This was
done to illustrate why some library users were dissatisfied
with the service provided.

Thomas Childers, perhaps the best known user of this
method in the field, has not only continued applications of the
unobtrusive method and written extensively in the field, but
has generated a great deal of interest in the method through
the workshops he had been running through the United States.
For example, in June 1972 he conducted a two-day workshop
on the subject that was sponsored by the Division of Library
Development of Maryland's Department of Education. The
participants at the workshop telephoned in a number of standard reference questions and discovered that "the service received was better at small, ill-equipped, poorly-staffed agencies than at larger, well-heeled ones."11

Another workshop in the evaluation of reference service that was conducted by Childers was carried out at the
Baltimore County Library's Towson branch. Participants
phoned in reference questions to local libraries to learn more
about evaluation of reference service from the patron's point
of view. The results were that "area reference librarians
satisfactorily answered only 60 to 70 percent of the sample
reference questions phoned in." A reporter for the Maryland
Library Association Newsletter, the Crab, reported that he
was satisfied with only three of the eight libraries surveyed,
and that responses ranged from "totally wrong, insufficient,
or at best noncommittal, to the thorough and brightly executed."12

A fourth study that was conducted by Childers using
unobtrusive measures was carried out in Suffolk County, New
York. The purpose of the study was to capture a realistic,
objective picture of reference and information service in Suffolk County's public libraries--a picture from the client's
point of view. Twenty-one questions were asked and their
answers were judged according to four scales of "correctness": correct, mostly correct, mostly wrong, and wrong.
Of the 1,110 observations, 627 received an actual "answer."
The rest, 483 observations, were either "turned away" by
the respondent, or the proxy was referred to another source,
or both. Eighty-four percent of the 627 observations that received an answer were considered correct.13

In this study, Childers further developed the use of unobtrusive measures to test the effectiveness of library reference/information services. In order to maintain the study's unobtrusiveness, each question was asked with varying content. This was done in an effort to forestall suspicions over the great frequency of test questions, should librarians communicate with each other about their reference questions.

The publication of Terence Crowley's and Thomas Childers's book in 1971 created a general professional awareness of the unobtrusive technique in the field. Since then, several other studies using the same technique have been reported in the literature. For example, Dorman H. Smith in 1972 administered unobtrusively a one-question test in twenty libraries in the greater Boston area. The methodology followed in the study was not very rigid. Neither the types of libraries used nor the answers he received were mentioned.[14]

In a Survey of Public Libraries: Summit County, Ohio, the unobtrusive technique was used to test the capacity of each library to provide answers to questions, both in terms of the correctness of the answers and general attitudes toward answering questions.[15] The findings of this investigation indicated that only about 30 percent of the responses were correct. However, the researchers stated that the difference in performance among the libraries under study were not great enough to be attributed to something other than chance observation. This made them conclude that "for these questions, the performance of the libraries was not different enough to lead us to expect differences on similar questions at other times." As for the attitudes of the respondents to the questions asked by the proxies, the study found that the respondents were consistently rated positively.

It is interesting to note that it was this study that first revealed that there was no difference in performance of reference librarians in public libraries whether the questions were administered in person or by telephone.

In another study of this type, a sample of public and academic libraries in Ohio was subjected to unobtrusive evaluation of reference services in 1972.[16] Two questions of the short-answer variety were used and each was asked of all libraries by the same person. Each encounter was also rated on the respondent's attitude in answering the question. The performance of the academic libraries was better than that of

the public libraries--five out of five for the first question
and three out of three for the second.   As was the case in
the Summit County study cited above, the respondents were
consistently rated positively.   The majority received ratings
of four or five, in a scale of one to five with five being the
most positive.

It is worth mentioning that no conclusions were reported by the researchers.   This might be due to the fact
that only two questions were used in the study, and a good
percentage of libraries included in the study were not open
during the time period when the calls were made.   The survey was conducted on a Saturday from 8 a.m. to 2 p.m.

Geraldine King and Rachel Berry, in their Evaluation
of the University of Minnesota Libraries Reference Department Telephone Information Service, also used the unobtrusive measurement.   The results of the evaluation indicated
that the Reference Division answered 60 percent of the questions correctly, 25 percent incorrectly, and was unable to
find answers for the other 15 percent.   The attitude of the
librarian was judged "pleasant" in 95 percent of the calls.[17]

In an extensive study published in 1975, the qualitative
aspects of reference service of twenty California public libraries were evaluated on the basis of their abilities to answer simple and complex reference questions and to obtain
library material known not to be in their collections.[18]   The
major findings of this study were as follows.   First, the performance of all libraries was surprisingly poor.   Only 15
percent of the libraries performed adequately on all three
phases of the test, and only half the libraries performed satisfactorily on two of the three phases.   Second, the failure
of the library staff members to perform well was a frequent
reason for the poor performance of libraries.

One important implication of the California study--and
this can also be generalized to most of the studies that had
used unobtrusive measures in their evaluation of library reference services--was that it rang a bell of warning to all
those involved in the professions.   It clearly indicated that
at a time of growing competition for funds, inflationary pressures, and the need to justify the importance of library services to those responsible for funding them, the prospects for
increased funding were not bright if the quality of performance
demonstrated in the survey could not be significantly improved.

The most recent study of the effectiveness of telephone reference service using unobtrusive measures was conducted by Marcia Myers.[19] The purpose of the study was to gain some insight into the effectiveness of reference/information services among types of academic libraries using peer evaluation.

The findings of Myers's investigation were similar to the results of previous unobtrusive studies in the percentage of correct responses on the overall performance test. The twelve fact-type queries were answered correctly about 50 percent of the time. Myers found that RASD's "Developmental Guidelines" had little association with actual reference performance and other measures of reference services. She reported also significant differences in effectiveness when the libraries were classified by type of institution. The median number of correct responses progressively increased from two-year colleges (5.0), four-year colleges with no graduate programs (5.5), four-year colleges with graduate programs (6.5), to universities (7.5). The two library independent variables that were closely related to accuracy of the responses were number of hours open per week and volumes held.

An innovation that Myers introduced to the use of unobtrusive technique in library reference/information services was the principle of substitution. This principle means if the test became obtrusive in a library, then that library was dropped and replaced with an alternate.

It should be noted that some artificial constraints were placed on the study, such as using white women as proxies, excluding libraries that had a predominantly black student body, application of the telephone calls during certain hours during the day only, etc. These constraints might have made the findings of the study of limited value outside its respective situations. Moreover, one might also question the type of queries used in the study because most of them were not curriculum oriented and they were not representative of most of the major subject areas that were taught in colleges and universities.

It seems, as reported in the literature, that researchers outside the United States have not had the same enthusiasm towards the use of unobtrusive technique in the study of library reference services. The scarcity of such type of research abroad might be due to differences in the nature of library reference services there. However, the present investigator was able to locate three studies: one was conducted in England and the other two in Australia.[20]

In House's study, which was designed as a small teaching exercise, students in librarianship asked the same question, a request for materials on a little-known illustrator, in twenty libraries. House reported that the failure rate was 60 percent.

> Twelve libraries out of the twenty in which the question was put were able to produce no information at all. Six libraries produced some information, and two were able to trace most or all of the information known to be in print, and to add new items.[21]

House came to the conclusion that variations in quality of reference service in that particular study was due mostly to interest and ability of staff, the lack of a methodological research strategy, and administrative structure of the library. He also indicated that the "available resources contributed in a small way to variations in answers."

It should be noted that the methodology of House's study was not rigorous. He did not identify the types of libraries involved. He used one query only, and that might be a reason for questioning the validity of his study. Nevertheless, the results of the study did indicate that the unobtrusive technique could be used on more than simple fact-type queries.

In a study of public library systems operating in Victoria, Australia, Ramsden used the unobtrusive technique to test the reference service effectiveness in these libraries. Eleven public libraries were involved in the study and nineteen reference questions were asked by telephone. The findings of the survey reported a mean probability of .49 of receiving a correct answer to the questions. In all cases library staff were overconfident of their success rate. They thought that they answered questions more correctly than they actually did.

In a study that was carried out over approximately three weeks in November 1977 in New South Wales, Australia, Janine Schmidt used the unobtrusive technique to evaluate reference services in three college libraries. Ten questions that sought general rather than factual-type information as was usually the case in similar studies, were asked in person by students in librarianship.

The findings of this investigation indicated that "in each of the libraries studied, the user making a reference inquiry has at best an equal chance of receiving the 'right' answer." Additionally, the proxies reported poor attitudes of library staff in the colleges answering questions. Moreover, the staff did not sufficiently negotiate the questions asked, and their performance showed poor question analysis and search strategy.

The results of Schmidt's study, like those of House and Smith discussed earlier, indicated that unobtrusive measures could be used on more than simple fact-type questions. Another positive addition this study had was the fact that the investigator inspected the collections of each of the three libraries studied to ensure that materials that could supply answers to the questions asked in the study were held in the library. However, the reliability of the study might be questioned because of the small number of questions and libraries used.

Conclusions

This review of the literature clearly indicates that efforts have been made to measure the quality of library reference services during the last two decades. Both obtrusive and unobtrusive measures have been used to determine the ability of reference librarians to provide answers to the patrons' inquiries. Both techniques make use of questions that are "contrived" in the sense that they do not represent the information needs of "real" library users. The major difference between the two techniques is that in the obtrusive measurement the reference staff members know that they are being observed and evaluated while in the unobtrusive measurement they do not.

Moreover, unobtrusive measures do not require the cooperation of the subjects and are nonreactive. That is, the measures themselves do not contaminate the objects being tested. Contrary to the high level of user satisfaction and the high degree of success reported by librarians in earlier studies, the results of studies using test questions and unobtrusive measures indicate that most libraries that have been evaluated to date are able to answer correctly just slightly more than half of the questions posed.

This review shows, among other things, that there has been some research on the relationship between some quantifiable aspects of the libraries and reference performance, but this type of research has been rather unsystematic, and there has been essentially no study that examined the relationship between the independent variables included in this study and library reference performance. Billy Wilkinson pointed out in 1972 that there was a great need for an evaluation of reference/information services in academic libraries using unobtrusive measures.[22] And such a point was exactly one of the major purposes of this research, since academic libraries have not received as stringent an assessment using unobtrusive measures as public libraries.

3.
METHODOLOGY

This chapter outlines the study's research design and methodology. Also presented are the procedures followed in selecting the research instruments, pretesting the research instruments, conducting the actual test, and treating the data collected.

In developing a methodology that described the relationship between reference/information performance and several other variables potentially affecting the quality of reference services, there were two studies that provided procedural guidance. The two studies, discussed in the review of the literature, were conducted by Crowley and Childers. Although these two studies addressed the need to know how correct the information disseminated by reference departments and personnel of public libraries was, the method of measurement developed by the two researchers could be applied to academic libraries as well as public libraries.

The two methods used in testing the research hypothesis were case study and unobtrusive measures. The choice of case study, which will be described in some detail later on, was dictated by the need to gain some empirical information on the several variables of the study. Additionally, this was done in an attempt to determine the logical interrelations of these variables, and the necessity to concentrate upon only a few representatives within the given universe of reference/information services for academic libraries. Wilkinson, in his study of reference services for undergraduate students, emphasized also the need for the use of case studies in investigating reference services in academic libraries by stating that

[169]

additional case studies of reference services for undergraduate students, as well as graduate students, faculty, and other inquirers in academic libraries, are needed to continue the detailed documentation necessary for developing in the future standards for the measurement and evaluation of reference services.[1]

With regard to the choice of the unobtrusive measurement as a major investigative technique in the study, this was dictated by the fact that the primary objective of this study was to apply the technique for the evaluation of accuracy of responses to factual questions coming via telephone to reference departments of certain northeastern college libraries. As indicated previously, the main advantage of the unobtrusive measurement technique is that the researcher is no longer known to be part of the action, and the subject being tested can be evaluated in an ordinary everyday type of situation.

As for the combination of the case study and the unobtrusive measures in testing the research hypotheses, it is believed that such combination of methods will reduce the possibility of sharing the same weaknesses of each method. In any evaluation, if different research methods are used, each will have its own methodological weaknesses, and the combined use of several should cancel out some of these weaknesses. Or as Julian Simon put it, "Several methods together may provide better and cheaper answers than any single method can."[2]

Research Design

The names of five four-year state colleges in the Northeast United States meeting the limitations imposed in this study were identified using The Education Directory, Colleges and Universities.[3] Such a small sample of cases was chosen in order to be able to collect more information related to the participants, their actual working environment and their work activities, and the unobtrusive technique. Thus, with a small number of cases it would be easier to study those libraries more thoroughly. The five colleges included in the study were chosen for geographical convenience. Library Statistics of Colleges and Universities[4] was then consulted to gain further information about the libraries in these colleges. This, the most recent collection of statistics available on academic libraries in print, covered only the period up to fall 1975. The investigator contacted the state's Department of Higher Education to obtain the 1979-80 statistics.

In addition to the statistics on library operations and the performance test used to collect data for the dependent variables, two questionnaires were constructed and used to gather appropriate data related to the library reference staff members of each institution, and the reference policies and procedures of the respective libraries. This information was supplemented by site-visits to the participating libraries. During these visits, observations were made of the working environment of the staff, as well as their work activities. The purpose of these observations was to gather supplementary data that might qualify or help to interpret findings obtained by other means. Every effort was made to ensure the anonymity of the libraries and reference librarians under investigation in this study.

Selection of Test Reference Questions

The decision to use only fact-type reference questions in this study was based largely on their reliability. This type of question required the least subjective judgment and the predetermined short answers could be measured consistently. In order to devise a test of "bona fide" questions, a number of sources were consulted for the selection of the questions and the help of experts in some other disciplines was asked in order to construct a few other questions that were needed to ensure the inclusion of most of the types of questions encountered by academic libraries of the type under investigation in this study.[5] Generally speaking, most of the questions used in the performance test had actually been asked in a library similar to the participating libraries. Powell's criteria were adopted in the selection of the questions that were included in the reference performance test.[6] This results in having a list of questions that:

1. Had factual and unequivocal answers.

2. Were not necessarily difficult yet were unlikely to be answered by every participant.

3. Represented all of the major subject areas (fine arts and recreation, history, literature, religion

and philosophy, science, social sciences, technology, etc.)

4. Roughly represented the questions encountered by academic libraries of the type under investigation.

5. Represented a wide range of difficulty.

6. Were, if at all possible, answerable with more than one reference tool.

7. Required a particular source or sources to be answered without requiring exceptional skill in the use of those sources, thus minimizing the advantage of a librarian with extra or advance knowledge about a particular subject.

In order to determine the number of questions needed to provide a valid reference performance test in the present study, an estimating formula was used, along with data from Crowley's and Childers's studies.[7] It was estimated that a sample size of approximately 165 observations would be needed. Since the number of the participating libraries was fixed at five, it was estimated that the limit of error of the percentage of correct responses from each of the libraries, averaged together, would be less than 5 percent, if thirty-five questions were used in the reference performance test. It is worth mentioning here that this resulted in having a study of reference effectiveness that had the most questions to a single institution of any unobtrusive researcher.

From a group of several hundred initial reference questions collected, most of which had actually been asked in reference departments of academic libraries, eighty-three questions were listed on a rating form. These forms were given to twenty-two academic reference librarians, who were asked to: (1) judge if the questions were typical of telephone reference questions posed in academic libraries, and (2) rate each question according to how difficult it would be to answer by checking the appropriate column under "easy," "average," or "difficult." Of the eighty-three questions, seventy-nine were judged to be appropriate. Of the seventy-nine appropriate questions, forty-three were considered "easy," twenty-one "average," and fifteen "difficult."

Based on the above consideration, thirty-five questions

that fell in the middle range of difficulty were selected from the list of eighty-three questions. Thus, it was felt that a good use was made of what Crowley described as the "principle of parsimony, seeking to make each question distinguish between the able and the unable."[8]

To ensure that the reference performance test would include a variety of fact-type questions, Van Hoesen's categorization of this type of question was adapted as a guide.[9] Although this classification was based on reference work in public libraries and was rather old, it was successfully used by Childers in his study[10] and should also be applicable to reference questions in academic libraries of the type under investigation in this study. The function of the scheme was to ensure some variety among the questions in the performance test; the questions used in the present study were designed to represent several kinds of questions that appeared to be curriculum related.

Van Hoesen's eleven question categories and the number of questions in this study which represented that category are detailed in Table 1.

The thirty-five questions and the accompanying rationales/additional information were applied to the sample libraries in the following order. (The number in the square brackets indicates the category of the question from Table 1.)

1. I need to know the percentage of U.S. crude oil imports that came from Venezuela in 1973. [2]

2. I want to know whether South Africa has signed the treaty on the nonproliferation of nuclear weapons. [3]

3. What is the normal boiling point of pure ethyl alcohol? (I think it is known also as ethanol.) [2]

4. Could you tell me the address of the International Federation of Women Lawyers? (I need some information about one of its programs to aid law students.) [6]

5. I would like to know the year that Dr. Bernardo Houssay won the Nobel Prize. (I believe he was an Argentinean scientist and he was awarded the Prize for his achievement in medicine.) [8]

Table 1

CATEGORIES OF QUESTIONS

Type of Question	Number in the test
1. Meaning type	3
2. Numerical or statistical type	3
3. Historical type	4
4. Exact wording type	2
5. Proper names	3
6. Addresses of individuals or societies	4
7. Books and publishing	4
8. Biography	2
9. Bibliographic verification of materials	4
10. Retrieval of factual, nonbibliographical information from any source	3
11. Geographical facts	3

6. (I wonder if you could help me) I would like to know the name of a general who was forced to retire from the Army after twice publicly criticizing President Carter's military policies. I think the incident took place sometime around the middle of 1977. [5]

7. How did Senator Williams of New Jersey vote on the Panama Canal treaties? (Adoption of resolutions of ratification of treaties providing for the transfer of the Panama Canal to Panama on December 31, 1999, took place in the first half of 1978.) [10]

8. There is a word that means "irrational fear of noise." Can you tell me what it is? [1]

9. (I wonder if you could help me) I have cited an

article and I forgot to write down the name of the journal. The title of the article was "A Definition of Irreversible Coma." It was a report written by the Ad Hoc Committee of the Harvard Medical School to Examine the Definition of Brain Death. Could you furnish me with the name of the journal, please? (I believe the article was published in the summer of 1968.) [9]

10. What is the title of the book that Jean Cocteau wrote on the Egyptian theater? (I think he wrote it while he was touring the Middle East with his troupe in the late 1940s.) [7]

11. Can you tell me who makes the PDP 11 family of minicomputers? I need the address of that company. (I believe PDP is the brand name of this series of computers.) [6]

12. When did President Lyndon Johnson meet Soviet Premier Aleksei Kosygin at Glassboro, New Jersey? [3]

13. There is a famous French novel that satirizes the philosophy of the German philosopher Leibniz. Can you tell me what it was titled and who wrote it? (I believe the novel was first published around the middle of the eighteenth century.) [7]

14. Could you verify the following citation for me, please? It is a doctoral dissertation. I suspect that the date is incorrect: York, M. W., "Reinforcement of Leadership in Young Adults," 1965. (I am not sure that the title is correctly cited.) [9]

15. I have seen a reference to a Jewish agency. It had to do with the transfer of German-Jewish capital from Germany to Palestine in the early stages of the Nazi rule. I wonder if you can furnish me with the name of that agency? (I think the name means something like transfer or exchange in Hebrew.) [5]

16. Could you tell me who among the United States Presidents were Quakers? (I'm interested in religious history.) [5]

17. How many white families were headed by females in 1974? (I am working on a paper about minority women who are heads of families and I need the figure for comparison purposes.) [10]

18. Who is the distributor of this film: I Heard the Owl Call My Name? I need also the address of the distributor. (I think it is a 16mm film.) [6]

19. Who were the publisher and president of the New York Times during World War II (1939-1945)? [7]

20. What is the meaning of "modus tollens"? (This is a Latin phrase and I assume it is an argument form in Logic/Philosophy.) [1]

21. Is there an English translation of Sartre's "Qu'est-ce que la littérature?" I need the bibliographic information of the translated edition. [9]

22. What were the birth and death dates of Nathan Banks? (He was an entomologist and I think he had the largest collection of Arachnida and Neuroptera in the United States.) [8]

23. What is the average salinity of the open ocean water? (I am writing a paper on marine animals.) [10]

24. What was the median family income in Elizabeth, New Jersey, in 1970? [11]

25. Could you tell me who wrote "The Revolt of Islam"? It is a poem. (I believe the original title of the poem was "Laon and Cythna" and it was renamed "The Revolt of Islam" later on.) [4]

26. Who said something like: The naive and the beautiful have no enemy but time? (It's just perfect for a paper I'm writing, some famous American or British author said it and I know it isn't new.) [4]

27. What is the address of Mexico City College? (Someone in one of my classes told me it is a very good school and has recently become a university.) [6]

28. I need to know the percentage of persons below the poverty line in Colorado for the year 1975? [11]

29. Who is the present president of Uganda? [3]

30. What are the names of the books that make up Lawrence Durrell's Alexandrian tetralogy? (The book I'm looking in mentions them but not their titles and I'm writing a paper and I need to know.) [7]

31. What is the symbol for a population mean? (If asked, you may say: My English instructor mentioned it in class and I'd like to use it in an essay I'm writing on symbolism.) [2]

32. Why is Connecticut called the "Nutmeg State"? [11]

33. What is another name for the circle of confusion? (It deals with applied mathematics/optics.) [1]

34. In 1977, the U.S. Commission on Civil Rights released a report called Window Dressing on the Set. It's about the treatment of women and minorities on TV. Has the commission published any study to update that report since then? [9]

35. I want to know whether Pakistan has signed the treaty on the nonproliferation of nuclear weapons? [3]

Design of the Questionnaires

Two questionnaires were constructed by the investigator. The first was employed to gather data about the reference staff members of the five libraries. The second was employed to collect data related to reference/information policies and procedures of the libraries under investigation in this study. The design and application of the two instruments are described in this section.

Questionnaire for reference staff members

This questionnaire, employed in order to gather background information related to the reference staff members of the sample libraries, is displayed in Appendix C. Nearly all the answers to the survey questions were of a numerical nature and were thus easily coded for subsequent computer analysis. Every effort was made to ensure the validity of the questionnaire items. Most of these items were adapted from questionnaires that had been used in data gathering of previous studies of library reference/information services. Additionally, a pretest of the questionnaire was conducted and administered to reference staff members in an academic library similar to the libraries that were being tested. The responses and comments of the participants in the pretest helped in rewording and improving some of the questionnaire items.

To guarantee a high rate of return for the final questionnaire and the reference policy questionnaire, a letter was sent to each of the five directors of the participating libraries two months after the completion of the reference performance test. In the letter, the directors were requested to participate in a study of reference services in academic libraries. Additionally, they were told that if they approved that request, the investigator would visit their libraries and interview them and the heads of reference departments separately, and distribute a short questionnaire to be completed by the librarians responsible for the provision of reference services in their libraries.

The five directors agreed to participate in the study and a time was set to visit each of the sample libraries. During these visits the questionnaire items were filled by each of the reference staff members in the presence of this investigator. In only very few cases, some explanations had to be made for items in the questionnaire. However, the field visits were very informative and seemed to provide ample opportunity for probing and cross-checking data. This method of data gathering was effective but costly. It helped the researcher obtain a 100-percent return rate. At the same time, it required traveling in a large geographical area.

Library reference/information policy questionnaire

This questionnaire-interview instrument, employed to collect data related to the library reference/information policies and procedures in the sample libraries, is displayed in

Appendix D. The questionnaire items were constructed based on other researchers' questionnaires that were used in gathering data related to library reference/information services, existing literature on library reference/information policies, and written reference policies of some academic libraries.

The questionnaire items were reviewed during the pretest by eight experts in reference/information services in academic libraries for face validity. The comments of those experts were very helpful and resulted in rewording and improving the questionnaire items.

As noted earlier, the questionnaire items were completed by the directors of the sample libraries and the heads of reference departments separately. The logic behind having two persons in each library answering the same questionnaire was that there were some questions that were related to the overall policy of the library where it was thought that the directors usually made decisions related to these aspects. On the other hand, the heads of reference departments were more directly involved in everyday actions of reference services than the directors of the libraries. That might make their judgments more reflective of the actual reference services provided in their respective libraries.

Pilot Study

The present investigator outlined and carried through a pilot study before launching on the full research project to determine the adequacy of data-gathering procedures and instruments. In the process of doing the pilot study, the investigator concentrated on the test reference questions that would be used: their selection, appropriateness, and validity. Moreover, this investigator was particularly sensitive to any reactive situation that might jeopardize the unobtrusiveness of the study, such as a reference librarian becoming suspicious of being tested. Also, the investigator wanted to determine if use of the telephone in posing the questions was natural enough in the academic setting.

An academic library that had virtually the same characteristics as the sample libraries was chosen as a pilot library. Ten proxies telephoned ten questions to the pilot library during its stated hours of operation between late May and early August 1979 at the rate of one question per week. The questionnaire that was designed to elicit data about the reference staff members was pretested in another library that had the same characteristics of the sample libraries and the pilot library where the reference test questions were applied. An analysis of the pilot study revealed areas needing refinement, pitfalls to be avoided in the proposed study, and insights for ensuring the success of the present study.

In regard to the methodology employed, the pilot study produced evidence that an evaluation of the question-answering aspect of reference/information services in academic libraries of the type under investigation in the proposed study using the unobtrusive measures was feasible. The proxies were told to report any indication of doubt or suspicion the respondents might have. This investigator was satisfied that the unobtrusiveness of the test was maintained throughout the pilot study.

Application of the Questions

In the search for an approach to apply the test questions, two ways were considered: the first, posing the questions in person, and the second, posing the questions by telephone. The in-person approach was disregarded because it was more expensive and time consuming. In the Summit County study cited above, Blasingame indicated that there was not any difference between questions posed in person and those posed by telephone.[11] Moreover, the pilot study conducted by this researcher proved that it was quite "natural" for academic libraries of the type under investigation to have questions by telephone. For all the above reasons, the telephone approach was selected as a means for the application of test reference questions in this study.

During the field visits to the sample libraries, the college catalogs, the library guides, and other relevant materials were examined for term beginning and ending dates, official holidays and the hours that the libraries were open, and the hours that reference/information services were provided. The application of the reference test questions started September 24, 1979, and ended March 7, 1980.

The questions were telephoned to the libraries during the periods 9 a.m. to 9 p.m. Mondays through Thursdays, 9 a.m. to 4 p.m. Fridays and Saturdays, and 2 p.m. to 8 p.m. on Sundays. All libraries were open for full service during these hours with one exception. Library 2 was closed on Sundays, so the Sunday questions were applied on another day during the same week.

In order not to bias the time-sample, timing of the questions was controlled following the technique used by Childers. Two questions were begun on Monday and Thursday of the first week, Tuesday and Friday of the second, Wednesday and Saturday of the third. Another question was telephoned on Sunday every fourth week. The cycle was then repeated until completion of the test. The first question was begun at 5 p.m., the second at 4 p.m., the third at 3 p.m., and so on, covering the hours stated above throughout the study.

After the application of questions was over, a Kolmogorov-Smirnov One-Sample Test of randomness was performed on the pattern of initial contacts with each library. The results of the test indicated that the sample was random.

Proxies were provided with "Instructions for Test Reference Questions" (see Appendix B). These instructions described the application of questions procedure. They were intended also to answer the most likely questions of the respondent, and to give the inquirers motivation in some cases. Additionally, the proxies were provided with response forms (see Appendix A) and were asked to fill the forms as soon as they finished their calls. The investigator was present during all telephone calls.

In an effort to establish the serious nature of the questions, the present investigator followed the examples of other previous unobtrusive studies of the effectiveness of reference/information services, in instructing every proxy to supplement his or her question with a rationale or other explanatory material. For instance, "How many white families were headed by females in 1974?" was followed by the explanation that "I'm working on a paper about minority women who are heads of families and I need the figure for comparison purposes."

Great care was taken in choosing the proxies for the reference performance test. The criteria for the selection of the proxies were: (1) they should not be out of the ordinary; (2) they have to be reasonably articulate (i.e., they have to be able to think on their feet); (3) they have to be attuned to the question of evaluation, i.e., they do not think that the use of this technique is unethical; (4) they have to be able to do it within my schedule; (5) they should be a mixture of men and women.

Each question was asked in every library by a single

proxy, "thus strengthening the likelihood that the inquirer is consistent in terms of aggressiveness."[12] The proxies included graduate and undergraduate students from various departments of Rutgers University, international and minority students, and university professors. The group comprised both men and women.

An individual orientation session was held for each of the proxies. The investigator explained to them the nature of the research and the purpose and the theory involved in the study. A set of general instructions were passed out and discussed with each proxy. The investigator and the proxies went through the instructions step by step. The purpose of each item was discussed. The proxies who did not understand a particular point were encouraged to ask for clarification.

A general picture of the other steps involved in the study was given to the proxies: how the questions were constructed, how data would be processed, and how they would be analyzed, so that they would feel more a part of the research team and respond accordingly.

Treatment of the Data

As noted before, success in answers was measured on the basis of the accuracy of the responses to a series of fact-type questions. The measurement used to determine the accuracy of the response was identical to Scale A from the Childers study. This scale and its code are presented in Appendix E.

As indicated in Appendix E, Scale A scored the responses on a simple correct/wrong dichotomy. Referrals, nonanswers, mostly wrong answers, and rejections were counted as wrong, along with answers that were actually judged to be wrong. Thus, on this scale, the sample libraries were being measured on their success in delivering a full, correct response to the request of the "client."

To increase the objectivity of judging the responses to the reference questions by this investigator, the judging was verified by four experts in the academic reference/information services. Additionally, the criteria for judging the responses had been established before the reference performance test was started. Generally speaking, the five readers were in agreement in their judgment of the responses. In the very few cases of disagreement among the five readers, the opinion of the majority was the final resolution.

The analysis of the data was done to provide a basis for either supporting or rejecting the hypotheses: there is a direct and positive correlation between reference performance in academic libraries and each of the identified independent variables; thus appropriate attention was given to analyzing the data so that the problem statement and the hypothesis could be addressed. After the data were collected and transferred to computer cards, the Statistical Package for the Social Sciences (SPSS)[13] was employed to perform various computations.

Every effort was made to ensure the reliability and the validity of the instruments used in data gathering in this study. As stated earlier, most of the questions used in the reference performance test of this study had actually been asked in reference departments of academic libraries similar to the libraries under investigation. These questions and the two questionnaires used in the study were judged as being appropriate to be used in the reference performance test by a panel of experts. Additionally, the pilot study suggested that such questions were acceptable to the reference librarians of the sample libraries and helped in identifying a few survey items that were considered as misleading, ambiguous, or poorly structured.

Nonparametric tests were used to determine significance differences. Spearman Correlation Coefficients, Kolmogorov-Smirnov One-Sample Test, and so on were used in the study. Because of the small number of the participating libraries (N = 5), the findings cannot be verified statistically and the results have to be treated tentatively. The statistics are descriptive and statistical generalizations cannot be made beyond the five libraries investigated.

Inferences from the data were not to be made; instead, these tests and other statistics were used as indicators (1) to examine possible trends and underlying patterns, (2) to single out the most discriminating independent variables, (3) to draw attention to unusual relationships, and (4) to begin to demonstrate the quality of one aspect of reference/information services available to the users of academic libraries of the type under investigation in the present study.

4.

FINDINGS: UNOBTRUSIVE MEASURES AND THE CASE STUDY

In this chapter, findings on the two techniques employed in the research, case study and the unobtrusive measurement, will be discussed.

The choice of the case study was dictated by the need to gain some empirical information on the several variables of the study. It was also used in an attempt to determine the logical interrelations of these variables, and the necessity of concentrating upon only a few representatives within the given universe of reference/information services for academic libraries.

The investigator, as outlined in Chapter 3, was fully aware of several dangers and disadvantages in the use of unobtrusive evaluation of library reference/information services, and it was deemed worthwhile to combine the case study and the unobtrusive technique as a means of reducing the weaknesses of each method.

As indicated by Webb and confirmed by Childers and Myers, the primary disadvantage of the contrived-observation type of unobtrusive measurement was the danger of being "caught."[1]   At this point, it is worthwhile to mention that no exposure took place in the present investigation.   The successful application of the thirty-five fact-type questions via telephone to the sample libraries was due primarily to the size and type of these libraries: four-year state colleges with graduate programs.   Additionally, this study used curriculum-oriented test reference questions and was able to build upon the lessons learned from the pilot study and the previous research of reference/information services using unobtrusive measures.

Reaction to the Instrument

The content of the questions

The selection process of the reference test questions used in the study, described in some detail earlier, resulted in thirty-five curriculum-oriented factual-type questions. These questions were typical of telephone reference questions posed in academic libraries of the type under investigation. Additionally, the detailed instructions in the application of these questions (see Appendix B) and the individual training of the proxies were helpful in creating an environment similar to the everyday situation that one finds at any encounter between the patron and the reference librarian. Throughout the study, no indication was found that showed a reactive situation resulted from posing the reference test questions.

The legitimacy of the inquiries

Every effort was made to select a number of "bona fide" questions that were typical of the kind of questions asked in the sample libraries. The strict application of the criteria for the selection of the proxies and the individual training session for each of them were helpful in the successful application of the test reference questions. Additionally, the rationales given to many of the questions permitted a controlled amount of information to be supplied by the proxy. The rationales also gave the questions more credibility. Proxies were instructed to indicate that they were students at the institution, if asked. And at the bottom of every response form (see Appendix A), there was the name of the town that the proxy was supposed to give if asked where he or she was calling from. This was very helpful. A good percentage of the respondents asked the proxies that question. At no time was there a refusal to answer a question because the respondent assumed it to be a puzzle, contest, or take-home examination question.

Of the 175 observations in the reference performance test, only sixteen, or 9 percent, were rejected. Seven of these "rejected" questions were at Library 4. The reasons given for turning away questions were: "too busy to look up through three or four indexes," "we don't provide reference services over the phone to nonaffiliated persons," and "I am alone at the reference desk."

It seems that the questions sounded so natural that even when mistakes were committed the respondents did not doubt the credibility of the questions. On one occasion, the proxy called Library 5 twice by mistake. At the second call, the respondent did not recognize the voice of the proxy, who had called only a few minutes earlier. Instead, the respondent told the proxy that "your classmate called ten minutes ago asking for the same information, which I was not able to provide." The respondent referred the "second" caller to the same resources to which he had referred the "first" caller.

The credibility of the inquirer's claim to service

All possible measures were taken to ensure the credibility of the inquirer. Nevertheless, some problems were encountered during the application of the test questions. Despite those problems, the legitimacy of the proxy's claim to service was maintained.

In the second question, in Library 2, after the proxy posed his question, the respondent transferred the proxy to another librarian who asked the proxy to repeat the question. The second librarian, in what was described by the proxy as an "interrogative manner," asked him, "Who are you? What school do you go to?" When the "interrogation" was over, the respondent advised the proxy to come to the library and added that they did not have the required staff to provide such service. The proxy was afraid that the respondent might have realized that there was a test going on. But the fact that this particular library had rejected only a few questions throughout the whole test did not support his suspicion.

A great percentage of the test questions, as indicated before, required call backs, and the problem of finding excuses for not giving the telephone number of the proxy had to be faced. The list of these excuses included: I am calling from work and I am not supposed to receive calls; I am calling from a pay phone; I am working on a couple of things right now and I don't know where I am going to be in the next few hours; my son is sleeping and I don't want him to be bothered; etc. No excuse was used twice. It is worth mentioning here that the respondents were not very demanding, and they were very cooperative and understanding for any excuse given by the proxies.

In many cases where a call back was required, the proxies were asked for their names. In such circumstances, they were instructed to give their real names. Although some of the proxies thought that the respondent would check to see whether they were students in that institution, the real reason for asking for the name was to leave the message under the proxy's name. Such minor problems would have been causes of detection if they were not taken into consideration by the investigator. It is the belief of the researcher that his presence at the time when the question was applied was a major factor in solving such minor problems as these and many others. The mere presence of the investigator might create uneasiness in the proxy, but this anxiety could be eased by making one's objectives clear to the proxy.

An important factor in maintaining the legitimacy of the proxy's claim to service was the fact that the sample libraries received about two hundred reference questions a week. Approximately 10 to 20 percent of these questions were by telephone. It could be conjectured that two additional questions a week did not add too much to the load of that library.

Communication among the sample libraries

Similar to the other studies of unobtrusive measures that were used in the evaluation of library reference/information services, communication among the sample libraries was one potential threat to the unobtrusiveness of the instrument. In the case of the present investigation, the threat was imminent since the sample libraries were members of institutional systems or consortia with other academic and/or local libraries.

The one indication of communication between two libraries in the sample occurred in question 12. The reference staff member in Library 4, after exhausting all the possible resources in her library, called Library 1 for information. This particular respondent asked the proxy when she called back whether she had called Library 1 for information. When the proxy answered "No," the respondent exclaimed "Wow!

This must be a popular question because someone phoned them too, for the same question."

From the answers to item number 5 in the Reference Policy Questionnaire (see Appendix D) and the results of the reference performance test, it appeared that the standard procedure of the sample libraries was to refer the patron to an outside resource when an appropriate answer could not be found, rather than getting the information for him or her from other resources.

Although the communication among the sample libraries was a potential threat, it was judged not to be a source of contamination in the present investigation.

Profiles of Reference Staff Members
at the Sample Libraries

As discussed in Chapter 3, the questionnaire that was used to get information about the respondents in the sample libraries had a 100-percent return rate. The results of this questionnaire (see Appendix C) and the field trips this investigator made to these libraries indicated that the number of FTE professionals providing reference/information services in the sample libraries ranged from three to eight. These professionals included part-time reference librarians who were employed either in other institutions or in other departments within the same library. In Library 4, there were eight people from other institutions; some of them worked at the reference desk four hours every other week. In Library 1, there were some staff members from other departments within the library who were assigned only three hours per week at the reference desk. While it is true that these staff members, especially those from the technical departments in the library, should be given the opportunity to have a direct contact with the patrons to be aware of their needs, it should not be done at the expense of the patrons.

In the interview this investigator had with those librarians who were assigned a few hours per week at the reference desk, some indicated that they often felt lost and did not feel that they were affiliated with the reference department at all. This was clear in two instances during the reference performance test, where the respondents were apologetic about the fact that they were not regular staff members. On one occasion, a staff member referred the proxy to another state college library where "you might find someone with brains who can help you better than me." This particular staff member told the proxy that he only worked at the reference desk for a few hours a week and apologized for not being able to provide more help.

The reference staff members in the sample libraries ranged in their ages from twenty-two to sixty-four years old, with a mean of 42.2 years. The percentage of male staff members in the sample libraries ranged from 16.7 to 53.8 percent, with a mean of 36.7.

All the reference staff members had a master's degree in library science. Twenty-one respondents, or 44 percent of the reference staff members of the sample libraries, had a subject master most commonly in education, history, economics, and sociology. There were two people with two subject master's each. One respondent had a master's degree in geology and another had a Ph.D in musicology. Most of the respondents had received their M.L.S. more than ten years before. One respondent received his M.L.S. in 1948, and the most recent M.L.S. dated from 1977. The average reference experience of the respondents ranged from 7.8 to 11.4 years in the libraries.

The reference staff members in the sample libraries spent about 18.6 hours per week on reference desk duty. The average minimum was about 10.2 hours per week, and the average maximum was about 24.2 hours per week. Some reference librarians spent as little as two hours per week on reference desk duty; others spent up to forty hours per week.

In answering question 12, which requested information regarding membership in selected professional organizations, eleven respondents, or 23 percent, indicated that they did not belong to any professional organizations. Eight of those cited the high cost involved in joining these organizations as a reason for not doing so, while another two mentioned that they did not feel the need for joining the professional organizations.

When the professional activities of the respondents were considered, only two respondents were found to be extremely inactive. That meant they did not belong to any professional organizations; they did not attend any professional meetings, workshops, colloquia, etc.; they did not serve on any committees; and they did not present any papers at any of the professional meetings during the past year. Otherwise, the mean of the professional activities of all respondents was 5.1.

Library Reference/Information Policies

As noted in Chapter 2, a questionnaire was employed to collect information pertaining to the reference/information policies of the sample libraries (see Appendix D). The questionnaire was completed by the directors of the libraries and the heads of reference departments separately. Respondents were asked to indicate how each statement reflected the reference/information services in their libraries by using a five-point scale that ranged from "never" (1) to "always" (5).

The major objectives of collecting the data about the reference/information policies of the sample libraries were (1) to be able to draw a profile of that service in these libraries; (2) to compare what the respondents feel is being done with the actual situation as perceived through the reference performance test and the field visits; and (3) to ascertain that the reference test questions used were typical of questions usually received in the sample libraries. The last objective will support the validity of the reference performance test.

There was no significant difference among the responses given by the directors of the sample libraries and the reference department heads of these libraries except on item number 13. The directors indicated in their response to question 13, which dealt with the preparation of annotations, critiques, etc., that it was "frequently" the case, while the department heads mentioned it was "rarely" the case. One explanation for the difference in responses might be attributed to the fact that the directors were not in regular, direct contact with the services of the reference departments as the heads of these departments were. A second possible explanation for the directors' response might be the phrasing of the item itself. It posed an ideal that represented the best practice and therefore was an attractive one to attain.

In order to determine whether there were any correlations between the number of correct responses in the reference performance test and the responses on the individual reference/information policy questions, Spearman correlation coefficients were computed. The four questions in the case of the directors that correlated at the .05 level or less for the five libraries were questions 2, 11, 14, and 26. In the case of the reference department heads, the five questions that correlated at the .05 level or less for the five libraries were questions 11, 12, 17, 29, and 40.

On question 1 of the questionnaire, the respondents were divided in their opinions regarding their use of a written reference policy in providing reference/information services. The two extremes were reflected in their responses. While two library directors mentioned that they "never" had a written reference policy, the other three directors said they "always" had one. The reference department heads were even in more disagreement than the library directors were. Two of them responded to the question with "never," one with "rarely," another with "frequently," and the last with "always."

On question 2, which dealt with the availability of the written reference/information policy to all library users, the three directors of libraries that got the lowest scores in the reference performance test indicated that they "always" had a written reference policy available to all users. The two directors whose libraries had the highest scores in the reference performance test indicated that they "never" had a written reference policy available to library users. It is worth noting here that what the first three directors were referring to as "written reference policy" in reality was only very general guidelines for library users. The department heads of the three libraries did not share the directors' opinion on what the directors called a "reference policy." One can conclude that the five academic libraries under investigation did not have a written reference policy at all.

On question 5, the majority of the respondents indicated that when their libraries' own collections and personnel were not adequate to provide a user with specific pieces of information, the usual procedure was to obtain the information from an outside resource for the user rather than referring him or her to that resource. This claim was not supported by the results of the reference performance test. Only in two instances did proxies report that they were told by the respondents that the answer was provided by another library in one instance, and by the psychology department in the other instance. Otherwise, the standard procedure was to refer the proxy to another resource, usually a public library, or ask the proxy to come in whenever the respondent was not able to provide an answer.

On questions 8 through 10, which dealt with the reference services provided to patrons not formally affiliated with the sample institutions, the majority of the respondents indicated that their libraries "always" provided these services irrespective of patrons' affiliations. The results of the reference performance test did not appear to support this claim. Very often the proxies were asked whether they were students in those institutions. On two occasions, two of the proxies involved reported that the respondents were interrogative. In the only instance where a proxy made the mistake of telling the respondent that he was not a student in that institution, the respondent told him, "We don't provide telephone reference service to nonaffiliated persons but you are free to use the library."

As indicated earlier, question 11 was the only question in the survey of reference/information services where the responses of both directors and reference department heads correlated at better than .05 level with the number of correct answers in the reference performance test. All the respondents indicated that the statement, "The user who comes to reference desk takes priority over the person who calls on the telephone," reflected the reference/information services in their libraries either "always" or "frequently." The results of the reference performance test appeared to support this claim. In many instances where call backs were required, the reasons given for that were that the respondents were busy with in-person inquirers.

Question 12, regarding the verification of citations furnished by users, was one of few questions that exhibited significant, positive correlation between the responses of the reference department heads and the number of correct answers in the reference performance test (r_s = .872, N = 5, p = .02). The two libraries whose reference department heads indicated that statement 12 "always" reflected the reference/information services in their respective institutions scored high in terms of number of questions answered correctly in the reference performance test. The other three libraries, whose reference department heads reported that they did not feel the statement reflective of their reference/information services, scored very low in terms of number of questions answered correctly. It is natural to infer from this finding that in libraries providing this type of reference service, the reference staff members would have more experience in citation verification than the libraries failing to provide that type of service.

In response to question 15, all the respondents from the sample libraries indicated that referrals to other sources and agencies were standard level of information service operation in their respective institutions either "always" or "frequently." This statement was supported by the observations made during the reference performance test. There, it was found that on occasions when the reference staff member could not provide an answer, he or she would refer the proxy to another institution or agency where the answer might be located. Most referrals, as mentioned earlier, were to public libraries.

On question 16, which stated that information provided to the user in response to any inquiry had to be as accurate as possible, all respondents mentioned that that statement reflected the reference/information services in their libraries either "always" or "frequently." However, as noted before, the results of the reference performance test showed that that claim had not been met, in that the answers provided to the users were not always the most accurate possible. It is worth noting here that this question was one of several questions that seemed to represent the best practice. Evidently, it was seen that way by the respondents.

On question 17, which dealt with the answering of telephone reference factual questions with information rather than with a referral to a source that contained the answer, the majority of the respondents indicated that this was either "always" or "frequently" the case in their libraries. The results of the reference performance test supported the respondents' statement. More than 90 percent of the questions asked during the test were answered with actual information. Only in a few instances was a referral made to a source that contained the answer. This happened only when a respondent, realizing that he or she could not provide an answer, suggested that the proxy come to the library and look through some particular sources where the answer could be located. It is worth mentioning here that this question was one of the few questions in the reference/information policy questionnaire on which the responses of the reference department heads were significantly correlated with the reference performance scores for the sample libraries (r_s = .866, N = 5, p = .02).

On question 25, the majority of the respondents indicated that the source of the answer was cited for the telephone inquirer either "always" or "frequently." The results of reference performance test gave evidence that this claim was not true. The library staff members did not volunteer any source for their responses in 56 percent of the total number of observations.

All respondents to question 29, which dealt with reference staff members' participation in continuing education programs, indicated that that was the case in their libraries either "always" or "frequently." The data collected from the reference librarians themselves (see Appendix C) did not support that claim. The reference staff members were asked to indicate what professional meetings, workshops, colloquia, etc. they attended during the past year. Approximately 50 percent of the reference staff members did not participate in any workshops, professional meetings, or colloquia during the past year.

On question 34, which dealt with the responsibility of the reference staff member to interview the questioner, all the respondents indicated that was "always" the case in their libraries. However, the evidence in the reference performance test did not support that claim. In many occasions where interviews were required to determine accurately what information the proxies needed, the reference staff members did not do so. The proxies quite often did not have a chance to spell out the "rationales" or the additional information that accompanied the questions. These rationales and additional information would have helped the respondents to determine accurately what information was needed. On the question about the address of Mexico City College, for instance, the rationale given would have provided a good clue for locating the correct answer. However, in the five libraries, the proxy did not have a chance to give it.

On question 35, which dealt with the degree to which the reference librarians took steps to ensure that the users' information needs were satisfied, the majority of the respondents indicated that it was either "always" or "frequently" the case in their libraries. The evidence from the reference performance test supported this claim. The respondents often asked the proxies whether their information needs were satisfied and whether they needed more information. This tended to happen more frequently when the respondents provided what they believed to be the correct answer.

In answering question 36, which dealt with the use of the whole library collection in answering reference questions, all the respondents indicated that that statement reflected the reference/information practice in their libraries either "always" or "frequently." There was no evidence during the reference performance test to support that claim. All of the sources volunteered during the reference performance test were items that were usually found in the reference collection. Sometimes, not even the whole library reference collection was used in answering reference questions. In two instances in Library 5, for example, the proxies were told to call back a few hours later because the reference staff member was alone and the science reference collection was in the other building.

The above discussion revealed, among other things, that the reference departments in the sample libraries did not have a written policy with stated objectives in providing reference/information services. This was not unexpected. In a 1972 study, Mary Jo Lynch found that "reference departments in many academic libraries are currently operating on a very informal basis."[2] The discussion also showed the need for such policy. A reference/information policy will enable the reference staff members to have a clearer concept of what they are trying to do and how they are going to do it. Evidently, the reference staff members cannot be all things to all people. Some thought must be given to priorities. Although each request for assistance is an individual problem, general guidelines for handling various kinds of inquiries would be very helpful to the library staff member at the reference desk. Guidelines would also create a situation in which there was greater accountability for effective reference services.

Additionally, the findings indicate a discrepancy between what the respondents (library directors as well as reference department heads) felt was being done and the actual situation as perceived through the reference performance test and the field visits made to the sample libraries. The responses to the questionnaire items revealed that the respondents were not fully aware of the real reference practices in their libraries. Most of their responses seemed to represent ideal as opposed to actual level of reference/information services.

5.

FINDINGS: INDEPENDENT AND DEPENDENT
VARIABLES

The data collected in this study were intended to measure the quality of performance in one aspect of reference/in-
formation services in academic libraries (the accuracy of response to factual inquiries) and to relate it to some of the
variables that have already been identified in the scholarly
literature of library and information science as affecting the
quality of that service. More specifically, in this chapter
the analysis of the data was done to provide a basis for
either supporting or rejecting the research hypothesis: there
is a positive correlation between reference performance in
academic libraries and each of the identified independent variables.

This chapter presents the data that address the hypothesis of this research and details the findings resulting
from the analysis of the data. First, descriptive statistics
for the individual variables concerning the libraries, the reference staff members, and the responses in the reference
performance test are presented and discussed.

Next, these variables are subjected to nonparametric
statistical tests. In the final section of this chapter, some
general findings related to the results of these tests are reported.

In data analysis, only nonparametric tests were employed. This was done because the sample size was very
small (N = 5). Thus, it was not possible to determine if
the variables were distributed with the normal law, which
was a requirement for using parametric tests.[1] It should

[196]

Reference in the Northeast [197]

be remembered that the use of such statistical tests in the analysis of such a small sample size did not permit inferences to be made from the data. Instead, these tests and other statistics were used as indicators to examine possible trends and underlying patterns.

Descriptive statistics, or frequency distributions where appropriate, are presented below for all the research variables. The major objectives for calculating the descriptive statistics were to produce detailed profiles of the sample libraries and their reference staff members, and to provide the data necessary to address the research hypothesis. In order to ensure the anonymity of the participating libraries and their reference librarians, it was decided to limit the reported information about certain variables to the mean, range, and the standard deviation only. It is worth mentioning here that the statistics for variables 1 through 6 related to the five libraries under investigation in this study, while the statistics for variables 7 through 13 related to the forty-eight staff members providing reference/information services in the participating libraries.

1. Financial Support:

Mean	937, 8 dollars		
Range	551, 2	SD	257, 553. 8

2. Collection Size:

Mean	284, 503. 4 volumes		
Range	155, 9	SD	62, 522. 6

3. Books Added + Books Discarded:

Mean	18, 1 volumes		
Range	17, 3	SD	7, 571. 9

4. Service Population:

Mean	8, 518. 2 persons		
Range	4, 6	SD	1, 701. 8

5. Number of FTE Professionals Providing Reference/Information Services:

Mean	5. 2 persons		
Range	5	SD	2. 2

6. Hours Open:

Mean	83 hours		
Range	26	SD	10.7

7. Age of Reference Librarian:

Mean	42.2 years	Minimum	39.5
Variance	6.5	Maximum	46
Range	6.5	SD	2.5

8. Percentage of Male Reference Librarians:

Mean	36.7 persons	Minimum	16.7
Variance	297.2	Maximum	53.8
Range	37.2	SD	17.2

9. Time Elapsed Since Formal Education:

Mean	13.1 years	Minimum	11.3
Variance	2.2	Maximum	15
Range	3.7	SD	1.5

10. Nonlibrary Education of Reference Librarian:

Mean	1.7 degrees	Minimum	1.2
Variance	0.1	Maximum	2.1
Range	0.9	SD	0.3

11. Reference Experience:

Mean	9.9 years	Minimum	7.8
Variance	2.3	Maximum	11.4
Range	3.6	SD	1.5

12. Number of Hours Spent at Reference Desk per Week:

Mean	18.6 hours	Minimum	10.1
Variance	34.3	Maximum	24.2
Range	14	SD	5.8

13. Professional Activities:

Mean	5.1 activities	Minimum	3.6
Variance	2.8	Maximum	7.7
Range	4.1	SD	1.7

14. Percentage of Test Reference Questions Answered Correctly by the Libraries:

Mean	56.6 questions	Minimum	46
Variance	1.5	Maximum	74
Range	28.6	SD	12.3

Certain highlights of the above descriptive statistics are worth noting:

The percentage of test reference questions answered correctly by the libraries (variable 14) was 56.6. This result is similar to the results of previous studies of library reference/information services that used unobtrusive measures.

The statistics for variables 7 and 8 indicated that the mean of reference staff members' age was 42.2 years. Almost two-thirds of the staff members were women. In other words, the test questions were distributed between the two sexes of reference librarians according to their proportion in the libraries.

Information related to the educational background of the participants was represented by variables 9 and 10. The question related to the professional degree (M.L.S.) was omitted in the report of the findings because all the people who provided reference/information services in the sample libraries had the M.L.S. The statistics for variable 9, time elapsed since formal education, indicated that the mean of years passed since the participants received their professional degree was 13.1 years. Examination of variable 10, non-library education of the respondents, showed that over 70 percent of reference staff members had a second master's besides their M.L.S. Besides his M.L.S., one of the participants had a doctorate in another discipline.

The amount of reference experience of the participants was represented by variables 11 and 12. On an average, the participants had worked as reference librarians approximately ten years. The mean of hours spent per week at the reference desk was 18.6 hours.

Lastly, information related to the professional activities of the participants was represented by variable 13. The mean of 5.1 activities indicates that some of the participants were twice as active as others. As indicated in the previous chapter, the library that had more professionally active reference librarians did not necessarily perform better in the reference performance test than the library that had reference librarians who were less active professionally.

Spearman correlation coefficients, with a correction factor for tied ranks, were calculated for all the research independent variables and the major dependent variable to provide a determination of the degree of strength of the relationships between these variables and to provide data necessary to address the research hypothesis. The use of Spearman correlation coefficients was dictated by the fact that the study variables were not measured on a linear scale. Therefore, the use of the more powerful Pearson correlation coefficient was inappropriate.

The results of the tests, displayed in Table 2, indicate that there is no significant association between any of the thirteen independent variables and the library's performance score on the major dependent variable. It should be remembered that although the research results can be discussed with validity only in relation to the five participating libraries, the findings of this study support the composite results of similar research. The use of Bayesian statistics, where a combination of prior information and direct sample evidence is possible, would allow the above high correlations to be meaningful since they correspond to previous research findings. 2

Because of the small sample size, even correlations as high as .67 are not significant. However, Table 2 shows that the number of FTE professionals providing reference services had a higher correlation (.67) with the major dependent variable than any of the other independent variables related to resource profile (variables 1 through 6). Next to FTE professionals was Hours Open, which had a .56 correlation.

The demographic variables, age and sex of the reference librarian, did not correlate significantly with the percentage of correct answers. Among the staff preparation variables (variables 9 through 13), the highest correlations were for Reference Experience (.70) and Hours at Reference Desk (.60).

As a whole, none of the independent variables was sig-

Table 2

CORRELATIONS BETWEEN THE INDEPENDENT VARIABLES
AND THE MAJOR DEPENDENT VARIABLE

Independent Variables	Correlation Coefficient for the % of Answers Correct
1. Financial Support	.20 $p < .374$
2. Collection Size	.20 $p < .374$
3. Books Added + Books Discarded	.20 $p < .374$
4. Service Population	-.30 $p < .312$
5. Number of FTE Professionals Providing Reference Services	.67 $p < .109$
6. Hours Open	.56 $p < .161$
7. Age of Reference Librarian	-.10 $p < .436$
8. Sex of Reference Librarian	-.10 $p < .436$
9. Time Elapsed Since Formal Education	.10 $p < .436$
10. Nonlibrary Education of Reference Librarian	.30 $p < .312$
11. Reference Experience	.70 $p < .094$
12. Number of Hours Spent at Reference Desk per Week	.60 $p < .142$
13. Professional Activities	.10 $p < .436$

nificantly associated with the dependent variable. In order to see which category of the independent variables was more effective in influencing the performance of the sample libraries in the test, additional correlations were calculated. First, the thirteen independent variables were grouped into three categories: the resource profile category, which included variables 1 through 6; the staff demographic category, which included variables 7 and 8; and the staff preparation category, which included variables 9 through 13. Within each of the three categories the average rank of items was added to result in a composite number for each group. Each composite number was plotted separately against the response variable. The results of the Spearman correlation coefficient test, presented in Table 3, showed that accuracy of response was associated more with the resource profile category than the other two. However, correlations were not statistically significant.

Table 3

CORRELATIONS BETWEEN THE THREE CATEGORIES
AND THE MAJOR DEPENDENT VARIABLE

Variable Name	Correlation Coefficient for the % of Answers Correct
Resource Profile	.50 $p < .196$
Staff Demographic	.10 $p < .435$
Staff Preparation	.20 $p < .374$

The purpose of the preceding discussion was to focus primarily on the associations between the independent variables and the major dependent variable. The findings did contribute to a greater awareness of the traits of the libraries under investigation in this study, their reference staff attributes and their respective reference performance. The cor-

relation matrix in Table 2 showed that the most important independent variables that had high positive correlations with
the major dependent variable were: reference experience,
number of professionals providing reference/information services, number of hours spent at the reference desk, and the
number of hours that the library was open. When the data
related to the thirteen independent variables of Library 1,
which had the lowest score in the reference performance
test, and Library 5, which had the highest score in that
test, were compared, it was found that there were consistent differences as far as the above four variables were concerned. For instance, Library 5 had almost three times
the number of FTE reference librarians as did Library 1.

Relationships Among the Independent Variables

The associations among the thirteen independent variables were examined in order to discover the degree to which
each pair was interrelated. It was hoped that such an examination would reveal any unusual associations among these
variables.

The Spearman correlation coefficients for the thirteen
independent variables are presented in the correlation matrix
of Table 4. Once again, it is worth mentioning that the fact
that with only five libraries being sampled, the variables had
to be highly intercorrelated for the results to be statistically
significant. The present results were considered with the
critical value of the coefficient as $\pm$ .729 at the .10 level.

As indicated in Table 4, the independent variables that
were more closely intercorrelated than any other variables were:
Financial Support, Collection Size, Books Added + Books Discarded, and Sex of the Reference Librarian. In the sample
libraries, the ones with more financial support had more
books, had more books added and books discarded, and had
a higher percentage of male librarians. The correlation between financial support and collection size was important because it verified previously held assumptions and the results
of Childers and Myers cited above.

The independent variable Books Added + Books Discarded, described by Childers as "the variable that is potentially of most value in describing the degree of change in the
collection, " correlated with collection size to a higher degree

Table 4

CORRELATION MATRIX: THE INDEPENDENT VARIABLES

	1	2	3	4	5	6	7	8	9	10	11	12	13
1. Financial Support	-												
2. Collection Size	.80	-											
3. Books Added + Books Discarded	.80	1.00	-										
4. Service Population	.70	.30	.30	-									
5. Number of FTE Professionals Providing Reference Services	.72	.67	.67	.05	-								
6. Hours Open	.36	.46	.46	.21	.24	-							
7. Age of Reference Librarian	.10	.50	.50	.10	-.20	.67	-						
8. Sex of Reference Librarian	.90	.90	.90	.60	.56	.21	.30	-					
9. Time Elapsed Since Formal Education	.10	.10	.10	.40	.31	.82	.70	.30	-				
10. Nonlibrary Education of Reference Librarian	.30	.70	.70	.0	.21	.82	.90	.40	.60	-			
11. Reference Experience	.30	.30	.30	.70	-.41	.15	.60	.50	.50	.30	-		
12. Number of Hours Spent at Reference Desk per Week	-.50	-.60	.60	-.40	-.15	.31	-.20	-.80	.30	-.10	-.60	-	
13. Professional Activities	-.40	-.10	-.10	-.10	-.62	.56	.80	-.30	.80	.60	.40	.30	-

NOTE: Critical value: $\pm$ .729, significant at the .10 level, with 4 degrees of freedom.

than any other independent variable in the study ($\underline{r}$ = 1.00 at the .001 level). This stronger association can be explained in that it is quite natural that a library that already had more books tended to buy more books than a library that had fewer books. In the case of the sample libraries, it seems that that was what they were doing. Moreover, with the growing financial pressure on academic libraries, librarians tended to be very selective in their acquisition and discarding. This was exemplified by the statement of one library director: "We rarely discard books anymore."

The Age of Reference Librarian correlated with Nonlibrary Education of the Reference Librarian (r = .90) and the Professional Activities of the Reference Librarian (r = .80). The correlation between Age and the Nonlibrary Education was not surprising and could be explained in that older reference librarians had been in service for more years and had a better chance to acquire other degrees besides their Master of Library Science degree.

As for the correlation between Age and the Professional Activities, it might be explained with a reference to the comments made by some of the young reference staff members during the interviews this investigator had with them. They remarked when asked about memberships in the professional associations: "Their dues are too high, the conferences are very costly; we simply cannot afford that." It is natural to infer that the older reference librarians who happened to have more qualifications or degrees and get higher salaries were able to overcome the financial obstacles. Also, some of the older reference librarians might have bought life memberships in some professional associations when these were available at reasonable prices.

Another important correlation that is worth noting is the one between Sex of the Reference Librarian and Hours Spent at Reference Desks ($\underline{r}$ = -.80). The negative correlation between the two variables meant that women reference librarians spent more hours at the reference desk than their male counterparts. It also suggests that male reference librarians in the sample libraries may have been given more diversified assignments off the reference desk than women reference librarians.

Relationships Among the Independent Variables
and the Minor Dependent Variables

Spearman Correlation coefficients were calculated for

the thirteen independent variables and the five minor dependent variables collected during the performance test: Number of Calls, Length of Time per Observation, Sources Volunteered, Attitude of the Respondent, and Sex of the Respondent. Descriptive statistics for the minor dependent variables are given in Appendix F, and the correlation coefficients are given in the correlation matrix of Table 5.

The variable Financial Support had significant correlations with Length of Time, and Sources Volunteered. This meant that libraries with more financial support took more time in providing answers and volunteered more books than libraries with less financial support. These correlations might be partially interpreted by the fact that the "affluent" libraries in the sample, as indicated earlier, correctly answered more questions than did the "poor" libraries. In the latter, the reference staff members, who did not find the acceptable answers, were more likely to take less time in searching for an answer and to volunteer the source used than were the reference staff members in the affluent libraries who did find the acceptable answers. Additionally, more questions were immediately rejected in the poor libraries than the affluent ones. This resulted in reducing the total length of time it took these libraries to provide the responses.

Table 5 revealed also the existence of a significant negative correlation between FTE Reference Librarians and Length of Time. This meant that in libraries with more FTE Reference Librarians, the reference staff members took less time in answering the test questions than their counterparts in libraries with fewer FTE Reference Librarians. This correlation might be partially interpreted by the fact that in libraries with more FTE Reference Librarians, the task of answering reference questions was divided among more people than was the case in libraries with fewer FTE Reference Librarians. Very often during the reference performance test, the reasons given by the library staff members in the latter group for asking proxies to call back or putting them on hold was the fact that the reference staff member was busy either helping another student, or that he or she had a backlog of two or more questions.

The most significant correlation, as can be seen in the preceding correlation matrix, was between Age of the Reference Librarian and the Attitude of the Respondent (r = 1.00 at the .001 level of significance). This meant that the older the reference librarian was, the more positively he or

Table 5

CORRELATION MATRIX: INDEPENDENT AND MINOR DEPENDENT VARIABLES

Independent Variables	NC	Correlations of Minor Dependent Variables			
		LT	SV	AT	Sex
1. Financial Support	-.46	-.87*	-.90*	.10	.20
2. Collection Size	-.41	-.67	-.50	.50	.50
3. Books Added + Books Discarded	-.41	-.67	-.50	.50	.50
4. Service Population	-.05	-.36	-.90*	.10	.20
5. FTE Reference Librarians	-.61	-.95*	-.46	-.21	-.15
6. Hours Open	.55	-.29	-.36	.67	-.21
7. Age of Reference Librarian	.46	.21	.0	1.00*	.50
8. Sex of Reference Librarian	-.56	-.67	-.70	.30	.60
9. Time Elapsed Since Formal Education	.82*	.15	-.30	.70	-.19
10. Nonlibrary Education of Reference Librarian	.31	-.15	-.10	.90*	.30
11. Reference Experience	.15	.21	-.40	.60	.70
12. Hours at Reference Desk	.67	.21	.30	-.20	-.90*
13. Professional Activities	.87*	.62	.30	.80	.10

*p < .05

NOTE: NC = Number Calls, LT = Length of Time, SV = Sources Volunteered, AT = Attitude, Sex = Sex of Respondent.

she was rated by the proxies. This result might be partially interpreted in that the proxies who were a mixture of men and women of different ages felt more at ease with older reference staff members than they did with the younger ones.

The above correlation matrix revealed that there was a significant correlation between Nonlibrary Education of Reference Librarian and the Attitude of the Respondent. This meant that reference staff members with degrees in other disciplines besides their M. L. S. were rated more positively by the proxies than those who had the M. L. S. only. That having a double master's did contribute to a better rating of that individual by the proxies might be interpreted by the fact that the broader range of education may partially account for the increased proficiency of the double master's over "M. L. S. - alone" group. This difference may also be related to the personality type of the librarians, as evidenced by the study conducted by Alice Bryant. [3] Personality factors of those who chose librarianship after qualifying in other areas of studies may be different from factors of those who chose librarianship alone.

The high correlation (. 60) between the Sex of the Respondent (or percentage of male reference librarians) from the reference librarian questionnaire and the Sex of the Respondent from the performance test as recorded by the proxies on the Query Response form indicates that the test questions were distributed between the two sexes of reference librarians according to their proportion in the libraries and that both sexes of reference librarians had almost an equal chance in terms of responding to the test reference questions.

6.
FINDINGS: THE QUESTIONS

In this chapter, the thirty-five inquiries that constituted the reference performance test of this study and their responses, in an abbreviated form, will be presented. The number and percentage of correct answers by question and by library are summarized in Appendices G and H. A brief discussion of each question is presented first. Following that, some observations on the inquiries as a group will be made. The final section of this chapter will be devoted to the discussion of the categories of inquiries and the level of difficulty of the inquiries used in the reference performance test.

Questions

Question 1: I need to know the percentage of U. S. crude oil imports that came from Venezuela in 1973.

Answer: 10. 6 percent.

Two of the five respondents (40 percent) found the correct answer to this inquiry. The two respondents who gave the correct answers did not require call backs. The first library gave the correct answer in four minutes, and the second library gave it in eighteen minutes. The library whose performance in the test turned out to be the best did not provide a correct answer to this inquiry, while the library

[209]

that performed the poorest, did. In the latter, the reference staff member suggested two sources and volunteered to send a copy of the page where the answer was located.

Question 2: I want to know whether South Africa has signed the treaty on the nonproliferation of nuclear weapons.

Answer: No.

Two library staff members, or 40 percent of all libraries called, gave correct responses. The two libraries that gave the correct response did not need call backs. The first gave the answer in five minutes and the second gave it in eight minutes. At Library 2, after a five-minute search, the library staff member in a very authoritative manner said, "We don't do research like that. We just don't have the staff."

Question 3: What is the normal boiling point of pure ethyl alcohol? (I think it is known also as ethanol.)

Answer: 78.5°C. or 174°F.

Five correct responses were received to this inquiry (100 percent). One respondent gave as an answer 78.3°C. This was considered a correct response after verification in the source she cited and checking with a specialist. Four individuals did not require a call back. Only one respondent volunteered the source she consulted: McGraw-Hill Encyclopedia of Science and Technology, Vol. 5, p. 99. The correct answer can also be located easily in almost any basic chemistry or physics source. The fastest answer was received in four minutes; the median length of time was 6.25 minutes.

Question 4: Could you tell me the address of International Federation of Women Lawyers? (I need some information about one of its programs to aid law students.)

Answer: 171 Safiliaishah Avenue
Teheran, Iran.

This inquiry was answered correctly by all the respondents (100 percent). No call back was required. The fastest response was received in two minutes; the median length of time was five minutes. Two respondents indicated that they had used Encyclopedia of Associations.

On this inquiry, two staff members warned the proxy that there might be a recent change in the address due to the new developments in Iran. One respondent suggested that the proxy check with the Iranian representative to the United Nations. The other gave additional and helpful information by indicating that this association was affiliated with the U. N. She gave their number, which she found in the Manhattan telephone directory.

Question 5: I would like to know the year that Dr. Bernardo Houssay won the Nobel Prize. (I believe he was an Argentinean scientist and he was awarded the Prize for his achievement in medicine.)

Answer: 1947.

Again, this inquiry turned out to be very easy, with five staff members offering the correct answer (100 percent). Three staff members did not require a call back. The other two required two calls backs each. The fastest response was provided in three minutes; the median length of time was 3.33 minutes. Two respondents did not volunteer any source, while the other three respondents volunteered one source each: Who's Who in America, Current Biography, and <u>Encyclopaedia Britannica</u>. In three cases out of five, the proxy was asked if he wanted more information about the question. One staff member even gave more information about Dr. Houssay without asking if the proxy really wanted that information.

Question 6: (I wonder if you could help me) I would like to know the name of a general who was forced to retire from the Army after twice publicly criticizing President Carter's military policies. I think the incident took place sometime around the middle of 1977.

Answer: Major General John K. Singlaub.

The five staff members, or 100 percent of the libraries called, answered this inquiry correctly. One staff member did not require a call back, while the other four required two call backs each. One individual gave the answer in five minutes. The median length of time was 6.25 minutes. Three staff members did not volunteer any source, while the other two mentioned <u>Facts on File</u> and <u>1978 Britannica Book of the Year</u>.

This inquiry required relatively more reference interview than any other inquiry discussed so far. The reference librarians asked the proxy two or three questions before starting to look for the answer. Such questions as when did the incident take place and where, helped them narrow the problem and led to finding the correct response. Generally speaking, the respondents sounded hesitant and pessimistic about their ability to find the correct answer. One individual said, "This is going to take a hell of a lot of time and we may not be able to find it."

Question 7: How did Senator Williams of New Jersey vote on the Panama Canal treaties? (Adoption of resolutions of ratification of treaties providing for the transfer of the Panama Canal to Panama on December 31, 1999, took place in the first half of 1978.)

<u>Answer:</u>   He voted "Yes" on the two treaties.

Two reference staff members (40 percent) gave the correct answer to this inquiry. The two respondents did not require a call back. The fastest correct answer was provided in four minutes; the median length of time was seven minutes.

This inquiry was constructed by the investigator to parallel a question used in a previous unobtrusive study by Crowley.[1] In Crowley's study, six correct answers (50 percent) were received on the question: "How did Senator Case (R., New Jersey) vote on the 1957 Civil Rights Bill?"

<u>Question 8:</u>   There is a word that means "irrational fear of noise." Can you tell me what it is?

<u>Answer:</u>   Phonophobia.

Reference staff members in two libraries, or 40 percent of libraries called, located the correct answer to this inquiry. The two individuals who provided the correct answer required one call back each. The fastest correct response was provided in six minutes; the median length of time required to get an answer was six minutes. One individual who did not provide the correct answer gave as a justification the fact that she "can't work backward from a definition."

<u>Question 9:</u>   (I wonder if you could help me) I have cited an article and I forgot to write down the name of the journal. The title of the article was "A Definition of Irreversible Coma." It was a report written by the Ad Hoc Committee of the Harvard Medical School to Examine the Definition of Brain Death. Could you furnish me with the name of the journal, please? (I believe the article was published in the summer of 1968.)

Answer: "A Definition of Irreversible Coma," Journal of the American Medical Association 205 (August 5, 1968): 337-40.

Three library staff members, or 60 percent of all libraries called, gave correct answers. One reference librarian provided the correct answer in twelve minutes without a call back. None of the respondents volunteered any source that was used to locate the answer.

Question 10: What is the title of the book that Jean Cocteau wrote on the Egyptian theater? (I think he wrote it while he was touring the Middle East with his troupe in the late 1940s.)

Answer: Maalesh: Journal d'une tournée de théâtre.

Two of the five respondents (40 percent) found the correct answer to this inquiry. Only one call back was required. The fastest correct response was provided in four minutes; the median length of time was five minutes. Two of the five reference staff members in the libraries called indicated that they used the card catalog in looking for the answer.

Question 11: Can you tell me who makes the PDP 11 family of minicomputers? I need the address of that company. (I believe PDP is the brand name of this series of computers.)

Answer: Digital Equipment Corporation
146 Main Street
Maynard, Massachusetts 01754.

Three of the library staff members (60 percent) gave the correct answer to this inquiry. Four respondents required call backs. The fastest correct answer was provided in four minutes; the median length of time required to get an answer was 4.25 minutes. None of the respondents volunteered any source that was used. One of the two individuals who failed to provide the correct answer mentioned that she could not find the address without the name of the company. The proxy commented on the way that librarian handled the inquiry by saying that "she was in a hurry and didn't want to think about it." Two of the respondents who provided the correct response offered more helpful information than required. They gave the telephone number of the company and the telephone number of the local distributor of the product.

Question 12: When did President Lyndon Johnson meet Soviet Premier Aleksei Kosygin at Glassboro, New Jersey?

Answer: June 23, 1967.

Three libraries out of the five that were called located the correct answer to this inquiry. The fastest correct response was provided in two minutes; the median length of time was 3.33 minutes. Four individuals did not volunteer any source where the answer could be found. The fifth indicated that she had called another state college library to get the answer. As mentioned in Chapter 4, this represented the only instance known to the investigator in which there was a communication between two libraries in the study sample.

Question 13: There is a famous French novel that satirizes the philosophy of the German philosopher Leibniz. Can you tell me what it was titled and who wrote it? (I believe the novel was first published around the middle of the eighteenth century.)

Answer: Candide, written by Voltaire.

Only one of the five respondents (20 percent) found the

correct answer. Three respondents required two call backs each. The correct response was provided in four minutes. Two staff members who failed to provide a correct answer suggested that the proxy look for the answer in a general encyclopedia or Encyclopedia of Philosophy. The most interesting answer came from a staff member who told the proxy, "I need author and title to find the work."

It is worthwhile to note here that one library staff member asked the proxy to call back the next day. When the proxy called the following day, the staff member then at the desk told her that she did not have any record of her first call. To add salt to the injury, the person at the desk the second time, without leaving the reference desk or consulting any source, suggested to the proxy to go to the County Public Library and added that that library was more prepared to handle such inquiries.

Question 14: Could you verify the following citation for me, please? It is a doctoral dissertation. I suspect that the date is incorrect: York, M. W., "Reinforcement of Leadership in Young Adults," 1965. (I am not sure that the title is correctly cited.)

Answer: York, M. W. "Reinforcement of Leadership in Small Groups." Ph.D. dissertation, University of Michigan, 1969. 116 pp.

Three of the respondents were able to provide the correct answer for this inquiry. Those three respondents did not require a call back, while the other two respondents who failed to provide a correct answer required two and three call backs, respectively. At the third call, the reference staff member who failed to provide an answer suggested that the proxy come to the library and look himself because he (the proxy) would be more prepared to find the response than she (the librarian). The fastest correct response took four minutes. All the respondents, including those who failed to provide the acceptable answer, mentioned that Dissertation Abstracts International was used.

Question 15: I have seen a reference to a Jewish agency. It had to do with the transfer of German-Jewish capital from Germany to Palestine in the early stages of the Nazi rule. I wonder if you can furnish me with the name of that agency. (I think the name means something like transfer or exchange in Hebrew.)

Answer: Haavara (the Trust and Transfer Office Haavara Ltd.).

Only one of the five library staff members (20 percent) was able to provide the correct response for this inquiry. The librarian who found the correct answer did not require a call back, and only one of the four individuals who failed to provide the correct answer required a call back. It took ten minutes to provide the correct answer.

The correct response to this inquiry can be located in most of the Jewish encyclopedias. In the Encyclopedia Judaica, which four of the respondents cited, a two-step process can be followed to locate the answer: first consulting the index under the heading Jews in Germany, and then reading the items under that heading in the encyclopedia.

Question 16: Could you tell me who among the United States Presidents were Quakers? (I'm interested in religious history.)

Answer: Herbert Hoover, Richard Nixon.

Five respondents provided the correct answer for this inquiry (100 percent). Only one call back was required. The fastest correct response was provided in two minutes; the median length of time needed to provide a correct response was 4.75 minutes. One library staff member reported that she used Facts About the Presidents to locate the answer.

Question 17: How many white families were headed by females in 1974? (I am working on a paper about minority women who are heads of families and I need the figure for comparison purposes.)

Answer: 4,853,000 families.

Only one respondent provided the correct answer for this inquiry. Three library staff members required call backs, including the one who provided the correct response. Two librarians rejected the question. One gave as an excuse that it was the policy of the library not to answer questions like this one over the phone. The other librarian said that she was alone and she did not have time to find the answer. The third librarian failed to provide the correct answer; instead she gave the figure for the year 1976. She also added some wrong information to that answer by saying, "Data not given by race in 1974."

Question 18: Who is the distributor of this film: I Heard the Owl Call My Name? I need also the address of the distributor. (I think it is a 16mm film.)

Answer: Learning Corporation of America
1350 Avenue of the Americas
New York, New York 10014.

Three respondents provided the correct response to this inquiry; the fastest correct response was given in three minutes. No respondents volunteered the sources consulted. One respondent said that she could not find the answer because they did not have updated catalogs. Another library staff member gave as a reason for not being able to provide the answer that she was too busy to look through three or four indices.

Question 19: Who were the publisher and president of

the New York Times during World War II (1939-1945)?

Answer: Arthur Hays Sulzberger.

Three library staff members provided the correct answer for this inquiry. The fastest correct response was provided in seven minutes; the median length of time required to get an answer was six minutes. One staff member indicated that she checked the New York Times Editorial Page, which they had on microfilm.

Question 20: What is the meaning of "modus tollens"? (This is a Latin phrase and I assume it is an argument form in Logic/Philosophy.)

Answer: Modus tollens is one way of reasoning from the consequence in which the falsity of the consequence implies the falsity of the antecedent, thus: If A is true, C is true; C is false; A is false.[2]

Only one library staff member provided the correct answer for this inquiry (20 percent). Two staff members required one call back each; another staff member required two call backs. The correct response to this inquiry took fifteen minutes. The only individual who volunteered any source was the one who provided the correct response: Funk and Wagnalls New Standard Dictionary, and Webster's New World Dictionary of the American Language.

Question 21: Is there an English translation of Sartre's Qu'est-ce que la littérature? I need the bibliographic information of the translated edition.

Answer: Yes. Sartre, Jean Paul. What Is Literature? Translated by Bernard Frechtman. London: Methuen, 1950.

This inquiry, which was asked by a native-speaking Frenchman, was answered correctly by four of the respondents (80 percent). None of the respondents required a call back. The fastest correct response was provided in three minutes; the median length of time required to provide an answer was 4.25 minutes. One individual indicated that she had used Books in Print and the card catalog in locating the answer. The one librarian who failed to provide a correct response mentioned that the library had the original French edition. When the proxy reminded him that he was interested in knowing whether the book had been translated into English, the librarian said he did not think so.

Question 22: What were the birth and death dates of Nathan Banks? (He was an entomologist and I think he had the largest collection of Arachnida and Neuroptera in the United States.)

Answer: April 13, 1868 - January 24, 1953.

Three respondents provided a correct response for this inquiry (60 percent). Only one of those three required a call back; the two who failed to provide a correct answer required one call back each. The shortest correct response came in seven minutes. The median length of time to provide an answer was ten minutes. The respondents indicated that they had used the following sources in looking for the answer to the inquiry: National Union Catalog, New York Times Obituaries, Biography Index, American Men of Science, British Museum Catalog, and the card catalog. One of the respondents who failed to provide a correct answer made a referral to the American Museum of Natural History.

Question 23: What is the average salinity of the open ocean water? (I am writing a paper on marine animals.)

Answer: 35.0 percent parts per thousand.

Four library staff members provided the correct response for this inquiry (80 percent). Only one respondent required a call back. The fastest correct response was provided in four minutes; the median length of time needed to provide an answer was six minutes. The sources mentioned in locating the answer included Encyclopaedia Britannica, Encyclopedia of Oceanography, and McGraw-Hill Technical Encyclopedia. The library staff member who rejected this inquiry gave as an explanation: "College librarians only do reference work that takes a minute or two." It is interesting to note that this type of response came from Library 4, where at question 12 the reference staff member who was at the reference desk at that time, after exhausting all her sources without finding the answer to the inquiry, called another college library for the answer.

Question 24: What was the median family income in Elizabeth, New Jersey, in 1970?

Answer: $10,282.

Four respondents provided the correct answer to this inquiry (80 percent). Two respondents, one of whom failed to find the correct answer, required two call backs each. Another respondent required one call back and the final two respondents did not require any call backs. The fastest correct response took five minutes; the median length of time for an answer to be provided was 5.75 minutes. Only one individual volunteered the source that she used in locating the correct answer: U.S. Dept. of Commerce, Bureau of Census, Census of Population: 1970.

Question 25: Could you tell me who wrote "The Revolt of Islam"? It is a poem. (I believe the original title of the poem was "Laon and Cythna" and it was renamed "The Revolt of Islam" later on.)

Answer: Percy Bysshe Shelley.

The five respondents all provided the correct answer for this inquiry. Only one respondent required a call back. The fastest time for a correct response was two minutes; the median length of time to provide a correct response for this inquiry was 5.75 minutes. The correct answer can be easily located in <u>Granger's Index to Poetry</u>. No respondent volunteered the source used in finding the correct response to this inquiry.

<u>Question 26:</u> Who said something like: The naive and the beautiful have no enemy but time? (It's just perfect for a paper I'm writing, some famous American or British author said it and I know it isn't new.)

<u>Answer:</u> William Butler Yeats.

No respondents were able to provide the correct response to this inquiry. Three of the respondents required call backs. Only one of the respondents volunteered a source: <u>Familiar Quotations.</u> He indicated that he had used the access points "time" and "enemy," which should lead to the correct answer in that source, yet he could not locate the correct response.

It is worthwhile to cite two remarks made by the respondents. One said that he was sorry that he could not give the old-time librarian service, because they were swamped with work. The second made a referral to a public library because, as he put it, "They would have more time."

This inquiry was taken from a previous unobtrusive study by Myers. The performance of the respondents in Myers's study was also poor. Only ten libraries, or 25 percent, found the correct response. The poor performance of the respondents in the two studies in regard to this inquiry might be explained by the fact that the quotation was not exact. The first word in the original quotation is "innocent" and not "naive," as is the case in the inquiry.

<u>Question 27:</u> What is the address of Mexico City Col-

lege? (Someone in one of my classes told me it is a very good school and has recently become a university.)

Answer: Puebla, Mexico.

As was the case in the previous inquiry, none of the respondents was able to provide the correct answer. Two library staff members required call backs. The median length of time needed to provide an answer was eight minutes. All the respondents volunteered the sources they checked in looking for the answer: The World of Learning, Directory of Consulates, New Mexico Telephone Directory, and International Handbook of Universities. A referral was made to the Mexican Consulate in New York. A reference staff member suggested that the proxy look in her phone book for the area code and dial "information." The failure to provide a correct response to this inquiry might be attributed to the confusion between New Mexico and Mexico.

This inquiry was taken from Myers's study cited above. In that study, library staff members in four libraries, or 10 percent of all libraries called, located the acceptable answer.

Question 28: I need to know the percentage of persons below the poverty line in Colorado for the year 1975.

Answer: 9.1 percent.

One library staff member provided the correct response for this inquiry (20 percent). Only one of the respondents required a call back. The library staff member who provided a correct answer needed two minutes. The median length of time required to provide an answer was 4.75 minutes. Sources volunteered included New York Times Index, Statistical Abstracts, and American Statistical Index.

Question 29: Who is the present president of Uganda?

Answer: Godfrey Binaisa.

Five respondents (100 percent) provided the correct answer for this inquiry and none required a call back. The fastest correct answer was provided in three minutes; the median length of time was 7.50 minutes. Sources used to provide the answer were World Almanac and New York Times Index. In one of the libraries called, the person at the reference desk, as she received the inquiry, exclaimed, "Oh, boy! The librarians are at a meeting right now." She asked the proxy to hold on. After four minutes she gave the correct response and she cited as her source, "two students from Africa who are here."

Question 30: What are the names of the books that make up Lawrence Durrell's Alexandrian tetralogy? (The book I'm looking in mentions them but not their titles and I'm writing a paper and need to know.)

Answer: Justine, Balthazar, Mountolive, and Clea.

All the five respondents to this inquiry provided the correct answer and none of them required a call back. The fastest correct response needed two minutes; the median length of time required was three minutes. The one respondent who volunteered a source indicated that she used the card catalog to find the correct answer. This inquiry, also taken from Myers's study, was considered an easy question by that author. In that study, thirty-six library staff members, or 90 percent of all libraries called, correctly located the response. The fastest correct answer was received in thirty seconds, and the median length of time was about three minutes, as was the case in the present investigation.

Question 31: What is the symbol for a population mean? (If asked, you may say: My English instructor mentioned it in class and I'd like to use it in an essay I'm writing on symbolism.)

Answer: M, $\overline{X}$, μ, or mu.

Two library staff members provided the correct response for this inquiry (40 percent). One of the two required one call back and the other required two call backs. Those who failed to come up with the correct answer did not require any call backs. The median time needed to provide an answer was 6.25 minutes. Two of the respondents who did not provide a correct response made referrals to a public library and to another college library.

It is worthwhile to cite the proxy who negotiated this inquiry. He said, "Before starting my calls I checked the symbol in the Mathematics section of signs and symbols in my Webster New Collegiate Dictionary, where it is under 'arithmetic mean of a population.'" The librarians' difficulties are somewhat surprising, although the "rationale," where it was used, was misleading.

As was the case in Myers's study, from which the question was taken, two of the respondents assumed that population was synonymous with inhabitants. Both respondents mentioned that the symbol for population was a "circle with four dots inside." Although the correct response can be easily located in almost any basic statistics textbook, the performance of the library staff members in the two studies was rather poor. In Myers's study, 30 percent, or twelve of forty libraries, found the acceptable answer; in the present investigation, as mentioned earlier, two out of five libraries, or 40 percent, were able to provide the correct response.

Question 32: Why is Connecticut called the "Nutmeg State"?

Answer: A nickname alluding to the alleged trick of selling wooden nutmeg as genuine.

Four respondents provided the correct answer for this

inquiry (80 percent). The fastest correct response was provided in five minutes. The median length of time needed to provide an answer was eight minutes. The respondents indicated that they used the following sources in locating the answer: Encyclopedia Americana, Collier's Encyclopedia, Encyclopaedia Britannica, and New Century Encyclopedia. The individual who failed to provide the correct response mentioned that he had checked Encyclopedia Americana, Collier's Encyclopedia, and several other sources.

Question 33: What is another name for the circle of confusion? (It deals with applied mathematics/optics.)

Answer: Circle of least confusion or blur circle.

Two library staff members were able to provide the correct response for this inquiry (40 percent). Three libraries required one call back each, the fourth required two call backs, and the fifth did not require any call backs. The fastest correct answer was provided in seven minutes. The number of sources the respondents indicated they had used was larger than any number of sources volunteered by the respondents in the previous inquiries. Sources volunteered included: Webster's Third Collegiate Dictionary, Fundamentals of Optics, Encyclopedia of Photography, Dictionary of the Literature of Photography, Dictionary of Science and Technology, McGraw-Hill Dictionary of Science, Concise Dictionary of Physics, Popular Science.

Generally speaking, the respondents were hesitant in dealing with this inquiry. At one library, the respondent, after accepting the question, said, "Neither of us has heard of it." He was referring to his colleague at the reference desk. He advised the proxy to call the next day when the science librarian would be there. Almost every respondent cited the title of the source and the page where he found it. This was rarely the case in most of the inquiries. It seems that the respondents, recognizing the specialized nature of the question, were very careful in dealing with it.

Question 34: In 1977, the U.S. Commission on Civil Rights released a report called Window Dressing on the Set. It's about the treatment of women and minorities on TV. Has the commission published any study to update that report since then?

Answer: Yes.

Two respondents (40 percent) provided the correct answer for this inquiry. None of the respondents required a call back. The fastest correct response took seven minutes; the median length of time required to provide an answer was nine minutes. Two of the respondents, who were able to provide the correct response, cited the Monthly Catalog as the source used to locate this answer. Two of the library staff members who failed to provide the correct response made referrals: the first to the U.S. Commission on Civil Rights in Washington, D.C.: the second to the U.S. Government Document Store in a neighboring state. Both gave the address and the telephone number of the two offices to the proxy and suggested that he either call one of the offices or write to it.

The third respondent who failed to get the correct answer told the proxy that there was no way that she could find out for him on the telephone. She added that the question needed a tremendous amount of time. However, she asked the proxy to go to the library and she recommended that he should look through the Monthly Catalog.

Question 35: I want to know whether Pakistan has signed the treaty on the nonproliferation of nuclear weapons.

Answer: No.

Two library staff members provided the correct response (40 percent). Four respondents required a call back.

The fastest correct response was provided in ten minutes. The median length of time required to provide an answer was seven minutes. The respondents indicated that they had used New York Times Index, U. N. Yearbook, and Treaties in Force in looking for the answer.

This inquiry had been asked before in a slightly different form (see question 2). The percentage of correct responses was the same for question 2 ("I want to know whether South Africa has signed the treaty on the nonproliferation of nuclear weapons"). However, the two libraries that provided the correct response to question 2 did not do so in the case of this inquiry, while the two libraries that did not provide the correct response to question 2, did provide the correct response to this inquiry. Only one library was consistently wrong.

This shows that there is little consistency in response to the same question when it is asked twice at different times. It is worthwhile at this point to cite Crowley, who also used one reference question with a slightly different form three times over a period of eight months. Crowley also came to the conclusion that there was little consistency in the reference librarians' answers to similar questions.

All Inquiries

The response

Of the 175 observations, 160 received an actual "answer," that is, a library staff member actually provided an answer to the inquiry that was presented. Responses to the other fifteen observations did not contain answers to the inquiries. The inquiries were essentially either rejected by the respondent or the proxy was referred to another resource, or both.

Table 6 below shows that the sample libraries gave correct responses to the thirty-five questions on the reference performance test 56.6 percent of the time. Appendix G details the correct answers by library. The average ratio of Correct to Wrong is about 57:43; the high ratio is 74:26 for one library and the low ratio is 47:53 for another.

As indicated in Appendix H, the greatest percentage of libraries answering a given question correctly was 100 percent; the lowest percentage, 0 percent.

Table 6

FREQUENCY AND PERCENTAGE DISTRIBUTION
OF RESPONSE PERFORMANCE

Scale A	f	% of 175
0: Wrong	76	43.4
1: Correct	99	56.6
	N = 175	100.0

The findings of the present study are consistent with
the results of other unobtrusive research on library refer-
ence/information services. As mentioned in Chapter 2, the
results of studies using test questions and unobtrusive measures indicate that most libraries that have been evaluated to
date were able to answer correctly slightly more than half
of the questions posed. Additionally, these results provide
evidence for the validity of the findings of the performance
test in this study.

Number of calls

As seen in Table 7 below, almost 59 percent of observations of a question required only one call to the library,
36 percent required two calls, about 5 percent required three
calls, and only one observation of a question required four
calls to be made to a library (.5 percent). The mean number of calls in 175 observations was 1.5. Almost 97 percent of observations were completed within one day. Only
five took more than one day to complete, accounting for 3
percent of all observations.

Length of time

The nondescriptive statistics presented in Appendix F
show that the mean time per observation was 7.2 minutes.
The minimum time recorded for an answer to be given was
less than a minute. The maximum was twenty-eight minutes.

Table 7

FREQUENCY AND PERCENTAGE DISTRIBUTION OF
THE NUMBER OF CALLS MADE TO A LIBRARY

Number of Calls Made to the Library	f	% of 175
1	103	58.9
2	63	36
3	8	4.6
4	1	.5
	N = 175	100.0

Sources volunteered

Table 8 shows that library staff members did not volunteer any source for their responses in ninety-eight observations, or 56 percent of the total number of observations. They volunteered one source in fifty-six observations, or 32 percent; two sources in eleven observations, or 6.3 percent; and three and four sources in five observations, respectively. The data on the minor dependent variables, presented in Appendix F, indicate that the mean number of sources volunteered by library staff members, per observation, was .646.

Attitude of the respondents

The proxies were instructed to indicate on each observation their impressions of the "friendliness" of the respondents. Though a highly subjective measurement in isolated applications, over the course of 175 observations it might nonetheless give some worthwhile evidence concerning the demeanor of the respondents. We might conclude that in the course of thirty-five encounters by thirty-five different people an observation is worth noting about the respondents' friendliness or unfriendliness.

Table 8

SOURCES VOLUNTEERED

Number of Sources	f	% of 175
0	98	56
1	56	32
2	11	6.3
3	5	2.9
4	5	2.9
	N = 175	100.0

The analysis of the comments made by the proxies in regard to the respondents' attitudes revealed that in 108 observations, or 61.7 percent, the respondents were rated positively and in sixty-seven observations, or 38.3 percent, the respondents were rated negatively. The average ratio in all libraries of positive to negative attitude is about 59:41, the high ratio is 69:31 for one library, and the low ratio is 49:51 (see Appendix F).

Sex of the respondents

Proxies were instructed to record the sex of the respondents. The data analysis showed that in 114 observations, or 65 percent, the respondents were female and in sixty-one observations, or 35 percent, the respondents were male (see Appendix F). This finding is consistent with the findings on the questionnaires that were completed by the reference staff members in the sample libraries (36.8 percent male). The above data indicate that the representativeness of both sexes was achieved.

Categories of Inquiries

As indicated earlier, the thirty-five inquiries used in

the reference performance test were selected from a group of several hundreds of initial reference questions, most of which had actually been asked in reference departments of academic libraries similar to the sample libraries. In order to provide another evidence for the validity of the reference questions used in the reference performance test, besides the judgment of the expert panel, an item difficulty index for the thirty-five questions was calculated at the conclusion of the performance test. The results of this item analysis were in line with the results of the expert panel. On the whole, most of the reference test questions that were judged to be difficult by the expert panel turned out to be so in the actual performance test and vice versa.

In his study, Childers applied a chi-square test in order to ascertain the degree to which the category of a question influenced performance. A major conclusion of that study was that the category of the question exerted an influence on performance on that question. The two categories that diverged most strikingly from the theoretical frequencies were "proper names" and "geographical facts" categories. The questions in the "proper names" category prompted more correct responses than would be expected under the laws of probability. The questions in the "geographical facts" category prompted fewer. As was the case in Childers's study, in the present investigation Scale A was examined to determine whether the observed frequency of correct answers differed significantly from an expected, or theoretical, frequency.

Table 9

CHI-SQUARE TEST OF PERFORMANCE BY
CATEGORIES OF QUESTIONS

	Performance (Scale A)
X^2	7.121
X^2 .01 ($\underline{df}$ = 10)	23.209

Looking at Table 9, one can see that the observed

chi-square value (7.121) is significantly less than the theoretical chi-square value (23.209) at the .01 level with 10 degrees of freedom.[3] Therefore, the working hypothesis that there is a discrepancy between expected and observed frequencies can be rejected. In other words, the results of the chi-square test indicate that the category of the question did not exert any influence on performance on that question. The differences in the findings of this study from that of Childers as it relates to the influence on performance exerted by category of question, might be partially attributed to the variations in their designs.

7.
SUMMARY, CONCLUSIONS, AND COMMENTS

The primary objective of this study was to apply the technique of unobtrusive measurement for the evaluation of accuracy of responses to factual inquiries coming via telephone to reference departments of libraries serving four-year colleges with graduate programs in the Northeast United States. The study also investigated the relationship between reference performance and other variables that had already been identified in the scholarly literature of library and information science as affecting the quality of reference/information service.

The two approaches employed in testing the research hypothesis were case study and unobtrusive measurement. The instruments used in data collection included observations on thirty-five factual inquiries via telephone, two questionnaires constructed by the investigator, and site-visits to the sample libraries.

After the data were collected, they were statistically analyzed. Since the study variables were not measured on a linear scale, Spearman correlation coefficients were used to test the research hypothesis that there was a positive correlation between reference performance (major dependent variable) and each of the identified independent variables. The relationships between the thirteen independent variables and other five minor dependent variables were analyzed, as well as the relationship between the number of correct responses in the reference performance test and the responses on the individual items in the reference/information policy questionnaire.

[234]

The purpose of this chapter is to summarize the most significant findings of the study, discuss some conclusions that can be derived from the findings, and consider the practical implications of the study results. At the same time, because no analysis is ever final, it should be possible to point to still more issues for future research. It is worth repeating here that any conclusions reached by an analysis of the data collected from the reference performance test conducted in the sample libraries, may be applicable to only those libraries studied, only to the body of questions contained in the sample, and only the academic year 1979-1980. However, as stated earlier, the results of this research, in many respects, agree with the findings of similar studies discussed in the review of the literature.

Unobtrusive Measures and the Case Study

Unobtrusive Measures

This study included thirty-five fact-type questions in the reference performance test; the most questions to a single library of any unobtrusive researcher. The results of this investigation produced evidence that an evaluation of the question-answering aspect of reference/information service in academic libraries of the type under investigation, using unobtrusive technique, was feasible. The unobtrusiveness of the test was maintained throughout this study, in contrast to other studies where "exposure" or "reactivity" of the instrument was a serious problem.

The successful application of the thirty-five fact-type questions via telephone to the sample libraries could be attributed mainly to the fact that these libraries, which were serving four-year colleges with graduate programs, received more than twenty-five telephone questions per typical week. Therefore, it could be assumed that two additional questions a week did not result in such an unnatural load that the reference staff members would suspect that something unusual was happening. Additionally, there were other factors that helped in the successful completion of the reference performance test. These were: (1) the use of curriculum-oriented questions, (2) the individual training sessions held for the proxies, and (3) the lessons learned from the pilot study and the previous research of library reference/information services using this type of testing technique.

The sample libraries gave correct responses to the thirty-five inquiries of the reference performance test in the present study 56.6 percent of the time. This finding is consistent with the results of other unobtrusive research on library reference/information services conducted in this country and elsewhere. As noted in Chapter 2, the results of studies using test questions and unobtrusive measures indicated that most libraries that have been evaluated to date answered correctly slightly more than half of the questions posed.

The present investigator believes that future research on performance evaluation of library reference/information services should be devoted to the investigation of means of improving the success rate in answering reference questions in all types of libraries. By now, the profession has enough evidence that a user has at best a 50 to 60 percent chance of obtaining a right answer to a simple factual question when he or she poses the question either in person or by telephone. Therefore, rather than doing more studies of reference performance evaluation, let us transfer the emphasis to diffusing the knowledge obtained from the studies that have already been conducted to the field and create a response from administrators and specialists.

At this point, the important issue is to increase field efficiency. The next point of research is to design and test strategies both in library school programs and for continuing professional education, which have as their goals increased accuracy and effectiveness of reference services. As an example of such strategies, it is worth citing Marcia Myers, who suggested that Figueiredo's recommendations for error prevention in reference work and remedial actions should be studied by those responsible for in-service training programs, continuing education courses, and library school curricula as well as by the practicing reference librarian.[1] To extend Myers's recommendation, Figueiredo's suggestions should be put to a field test, preferably using a "before" and "after" experimental design.

Profiles of Reference Staff Members in the Sample Libraries

The number of FTE professionals providing reference/information services in the sample libraries ranged from three to eight per institution and in age from thirty-two to sixty-four years, with a mean of 42.2 years. The percentage of male reference staff members in the participating libraries was from 16.7 to 53.8 percent, with a mean of 36.7 percent. All reference staff members had master's degrees in library science. Forty percent of them had a subject master's most commonly in education, history, economics, or sociology. Most of the respondents had received their M. L. S. more than ten years before. The average reference experience of the respondents ranged from 7.8 to 11.4 years. They usually spent an average of 18.6 hours per week on reference desk duty. About 75 percent of the respondents were members of at least one professional organization, attended two or three professional meetings, workshops, colloquia, or other activity during the past year.

Library Reference/Information Policies

As noted in Chapter 3, the analysis of the responses to the library reference/information policy questionnaire revealed that the reference departments in the sample libraries did not have a written policy with stated objectives in providing reference/information services. That analysis also showed the existence of a wide discrepancy between what the library directors, as well as reference department heads, felt was being done and the actual situation as measured through the reference performance test. The responses to the questionnaire items revealed also that the respondents (library directors and reference department heads) seemed not to be fully aware of the real reference practices in their libraries. Most of their responses seemed to represent ideal as opposed to actual level of reference/information services.

The above picture might be one of the reasons for poor performance in the reference performance test. This suggests the need for reference/information service policy for academic libraries. Such a written policy would enable the reference staff members to have a clearer concept of what they are trying to do and how they are to do it. A reference policy, based on RASD Guidelines[2] and tailored to the special needs of that particular library, could be helpful to the library staff member at the reference desk in handling various kinds of inquiries. This policy could assist also in creating a situation in which there was greater accountability for effective reference services. It could also help if it were put into practice in eliminating the difference between the perceived ideals and the practice, mentioned earlier.

Independent and Dependent Variables

The results of the statistical analysis indicated that there was no significant association between any of the thirteen independent variables and the library's performance score on the major dependent variable. However, because of the small sample size, the variables had to be highly correlated for the results to be statistically significant. These four variables with the highest correlations were as follows:

1. Reference Experience of the Participants had the highest correlation coefficient with the major dependent variable (.70) among all thirteen variables. On an average, the participants had worked as reference librarians approximately ten years.

2. A second important variable was the Number of the FTE Professionals Providing Reference/Information Services in the Participating Libraries, and it was found to have a mean of 5.2 professionals. The correlation coefficient between this variable and the percentage of reference questions answered correctly was .67.

3. The third important variable was Number of Hours Spent at Reference Desk by the Participants. The mean for this variable was 18.6 hours. It was found that the correlation coefficient between this variable and the percentage of reference questions answered correctly was .60.

4. The fourth important variable in this list was the Number of Hours That the Library Was Open. The mean for this variable was eighty-three hours. The correlation coefficient between this variable and the percentage of the test reference questions answered correctly was .56. "Hours Open" was highly correlated with the number of correct answers in both Myers's and Childers's studies.

5. When all independent variables were grouped into three categories, it was found that the resource profile category was more highly correlated with the percentage of correct responses than the other two categories: the staff demographic and the staff preparation categories.

The Questions

The "percentage of test reference questions answered correctly" (56.6 percent) in this study is similar to the results of previous studies of library reference/information services using unobtrusive measures. Almost 59 percent of observations of questions required only one call to the library, 36 percent required two calls, about 5 percent required three calls, and only one observation of a question required four calls to be made to the library. The mean time per observation was about seven minutes. The minimum time recorded for an answer to be given was less than a minute. The maximum was twenty-eight minutes.

Library staff members did not volunteer any source for their responses 56 percent of the time. The library staff members' attitude was rated positively by the proxies 61.7 percent of the time.

In this study, reasons for failure to answer questions could be attributed to:

1. The library staff did not take advantage of the wide resources available in their own libraries or other library resources at local, state, and national levels.

2. The library staff did not make use of subject specialists within the broader institutions or outside them.

3. The library staff claim that they did not have time to answer the question.

4. The library staff did not know how to use, or misinterpreted the information given in some of the sources.

5. What could be explained as "attitude" was another too frequent cause of the staff failure. Many of the proxies reported the staff member's lack of interest in the question, lack of desire to serve, and unwillingness to help.

6. The fact that the reference staff member was working under pressure, especially when he or she put the telephone inquirer on hold.

As noted earlier, the results of this study showed that there was at best 56.6 percent chance of obtaining a right answer to a question. The most important and far-reaching implication of such results is for continued library viability. If library clients become aware of the fact that their inquiries are answered incorrectly, they might very well lose confidence in the reference services of the specific library, and perhaps in libraries in general. At the very least, their level of confidence in libraries might be reduced.

Another important implication of this study is as a warning bell to all those involved in the profession. It clearly indicates that at a time of growing competition for funds, inflationary pressures, and the need to justify the importance of academic library reference services to those responsible for funding them, the prospects of increased funding will not be bright if the quality of performance demonstrated in this study cannot be significantly improved. Clearly, greater accountability is called for.

A third and final important implication of this study is the extent to which it can be generalized. It sheds light on the fact shown to be true in the case of public library reference services through the works of Crowley and Childers. Now it is shown to be also the case in academic libraries. In this age of "information explosion," with a multitude of resource centers, it will be unrealistic to assume that a large number of library clients will seek to meet their information needs where the expectation of success is no higher than 50 to 60 percent, as is shown to be the case in this study and most other unobtrusive studies of library reference services.

If we can draw some general recommendations based on the results, we can suggest:

1. Continuing education programs for reference staff members in the use of information sources and information handling techniques, specifically regular training sessions in using newly arrived reference sources. This is considered to be a kind of awareness activity to familiarize the staff with a variety of information within sources and how to use them.

   Currently, the education of the reference librarian is considered complete upon the reception of the M.L.S. This reference performance test suggests the necessity for greater concentration of training on the job through staff development activities.

2. Many authors have repeated time and again that the attitude of the individual reference librarian, his or her interest, desire, willingness to help, is the most important factor influencing the caliber of reference services. This suggestion should be taken seriously by the practicing reference librarian. His or her proper attitude in answering reference inquiries is a professional responsibility and must be considered as such.

3. The study showed the need for reference staff members to correlate more effectively with other agencies at local, state, and national levels, and with subject specialists inside and outside their own institutions.

4. The study revealed that one reason of failure in the reference performance test might be attributed to the pressure under which the reference staff member found himself. Putting the telephone reference inquirer on hold was not an ideal situation to work under. It is the belief of this investigator that the best solution to this problem is for the reference staff member to take all the information necessary about the question from the patron and ask him or her to call back at an appropriate time, or call the patron back with the answer. An additional ideal solution might be to staff telephone reference services separately from desk reference services.

5. It is apparent that one of Childers's suggestions of ten years ago needs reiteration. He suggested considering altering reference/information policy in such a way as to limit responses to certain kinds of questions or to certain times of day when resources for answering (i.e., staff) are available.[3]

6. Although both directors of the sample libraries and reference department heads mentioned that reference desks were always manned by professionals, there was considerable evidence to indicate that answering telephone questions was often left to technical assistants and student assistants.

Suggestions for Further Research

Additional research related to methodological aspects of the research design and instrument is needed.

1. For reasons mentioned earlier, the study had to concentrate on only a few libraries. This resulted in a small sample size. As a consequence, the variables had to be highly correlated for the results to be statistically significant. Another study with a larger sample than the present study would produce generalizable results.

2. This researcher suggests that the present study will be replicated with some alterations in the research design in such a way that the researcher will be able to identify the respondent to each question. The unit of analysis should be put on the personal and professional attributes, such as the ability to communicate, motivation, etc. This would help in identifying some of the basic characteristics and qualifications of successful academic reference librarians.

3. Additional unobtrusive studies of other aspects of library reference services, besides the accuracy of response to factual inquiries, are needed to continue the detailed documentation necessary for developing the future standards of reference/information performance.

4. Another recommendation for the development of unobtrusive studies is to make use of the present technology in carrying out research. For example, equipment to record the telephone calls might be used. Such means would help the researcher in having transcripts of calls rather than depending on the memory of the proxy in recording and reporting the reference encounter. However, this recommendation is fraught with legal and ethical complications.

5. A total examination of the conditions under which academic reference services are given is another area of research that needs further exploration. The concept of the reference desk located in the open might be a bad idea, assuming that we want

the answers to be accurate. It is possible that we have emphasized accessibility of the reference librarians at the expense of creating conditions in which questions may be answered with great accuracy. A study can be conducted where we have a controlled group of libraries and experimental group where we change the working conditions of reference librarians to see whether that would have an effect on the reference performance. The suggested changes in the working conditions of the reference librarians include for example, changing the physical conditions by giving the reference librarians private offices, and enhancing communication among reference librarians at a given library to increase the sense of responsibility toward the client.

6. We should devote more time and effort to investigating means of improving the current poor reference performance that proved to be the case in most of the unobtrusive studies to date.

Appendix A

QUERY RESPONSE FORM

Query No.: _____

Inquirer: _____

Library: _____

_____

_____ Phone: _____

The Question:

If you are asked where you are calling from, please answer:

_____

Date _____

Begin call _____   End call _____

Response _____

_____

_____

_____

Refusal to answer (if applicable) _____

Referral (if made) _____

Replace call _____

Sex of respondent: Male _____   Female _____

2nd Call

Date _____

Begin call _____   End call _____

Response _____

_____

_____

_____

Referral (if made) _____

Source (if given) _____

Sex of respondent: Male _____   Female _____

Comments:

_____ (Please record any other observation you have about this query to this library here):

_____

_____

_____

[245]

Appendix B

INSTRUCTIONS FOR TEST REFERENCE QUESTIONS

1. Ask the question within the time block indicated on the form and record: the beginning time, the completion time, and the date.

2. The questions should be put in your own words and posed consistently to all respondents in terms of the amount of information accompanying the question, your tone of voice, and your rationale (the information given in parentheses).

3. The rationale for some questions, given in parentheses, should be presented only when it seems necessary. Present it as a serious question, not as one satisfying mere curiosity or aiming to help with a quiz or homework, etc.

4. If you are asked where you are calling from, please mention the name of the city written on the first page of the query response form. (That way the respondent will assume that you are a student at that college or that you reside in the area served by that library.)

5. If the respondent suggests calling you back, explain that it is easier for you to call the library back. (The respondent might become suspicious if he knew that the call was long distance.)

6. Using the space available for Response, record the answer(s) given, reference source(s) used, and/or any libraries or persons consulted by the respondent.

7. In the Comments Section, in addition to providing your observation about the query to this library, please indicate your feeling about the respondent's attitude and personality. For example: friendly, hostile, favorable, unfavorable, etc.

If there are problems, questions, confusing instructions, please feel free to call me at either of the following numbers:

Home:
Office:

Thank you.

Appendix C

QUESTIONNAIRE FOR REFERENCE STAFF MEMBERS

1. Library: _____ 2. Date: _____

3. Title or Position: _____

4. Department or Division: _____

5. Age: _____ 6. Sex: M _____ F _____

7. Circle the educational degrees you have received:

   (a) Bachelor's (b) M. L. S. (c) Subject Master's

   (d) Doctorate _____

8. Year in which you received your professional degree in library/information science: _____

9. If you are currently taking courses toward another degree, how many hours have you completed? _____

   What is the degree? _____

10. Number of years of experience as a reference librarian:

    _____

11. Number of years of professional library experience:

    _____

12. In which of the following library organizations do you hold personal membership:

    ALA (American Library Association) _____

    RASD (Reference & Adult Services Division) _____

    ACRL (Association of College & Research Libraries _____

    ASIS (American Society for Information Science) _____

[247]

SLA (Special Libraries Association) _____

NJLA (New Jersey Library Association) _____

Other (Please Specify) _____

13. If you are a member of a professional organization, are you currently serving on any committees? Which ones?

_____

_____

_____

_____

14. Specifically, what professional meetings, workshops, colloquia, etc. did you attend during the past year?

_____

_____

_____

15. Have you presented any papers, given speeches, or served on panels at any of those meetings during the past year? If yes, which meetings? _____

_____

_____

16. Number of hours you spend per week on reference/information desk duty: _____

17. Number of hours you spend per week in performing other assigned library tasks: _____

Appendix D

SURVEY OF ACADEMIC LIBRARY REFERENCE/
INFORMATION SERVICES

Instructions

This questionnaire should be completed by the director
of the library and the head of reference department separately.
Answer each question about your services in terms of what
services are currently provided. DO NOT include services
you planned for the future.

Listed below are several statements pertaining to ref-
erence/information services. Please indicate how each statement relates to services in your library by writing the appropriate number (1 through 5) in the box provided prior to each
statement using the following key list:

1. Never

2. Rarely

3. Occasionally

4. Frequently

5. Always

General Information (Policies and Procedures)

[ ] 1. A written service policy with stated objectives is
used in providing reference/information services.

[ ] 2. This service policy is available to all library users.

[ ] 3. There is formal cooperation between my library and
other libraries or information agencies at local,
regional, state, and national levels.

[ ] 4. Assistance to users, apart from "ready reference"
kinds of inquiries, ordinarily takes the form of providing guidance in the pursuit of information rather
than providing the information itself.

[ ] 5. When your library's own collection and personnel
are not adequate to provide a user with specific

[249]

pieces of information, your library acts as his direct agent to obtain the information, in contrast to merely referring the user to an outside resource.

[ ] 6. The library maintains a file of community resources and consultants.

[ ] 7. The accuracy of the source used to answer reference/information questions is the responsibility of the user.

[ ] 8. The library has no responsibility to patrons not formally affiliated with the college.

[ ] 9. Users are given routine reference service without respect to their affiliations.

[ ] 10. In the case of a time-consuming inquiry, if a library user is not affiliated with your college, assistance beyond the routine reference service is not given.

[ ] 11. The user who comes to reference desk takes priority over the person who calls on the telephone.

[ ] 12. The reference department verifies, completes, or corrects bibliographic citations furnished by users.

[ ] 13. The reference department prepares annotations, critiques, etc. as aids for the user in screening a long list of citations.

[ ] 14. The reference department provides Selective Dissemination of Information Services which bring new publications to the attention of the user.

[ ] 15. Referrals to other sources and agencies are a standard level of information service operation in my library.

[ ] 16. Information provided to the user in response to any inquiry must be as accurate as possible.

[ ] 17. Fact-type* questions received via telephone are an-

---

*Fact-type questions are questions which require a simple answer that may be found in one source although the library staff member may have to look in more than one source before the answer is located.

swered with information rather than with a referral to a source that contains the answer.

[ ] 18.   Answers to fact-type questions are verified in more than one source for accuracy and recent changes.

[ ] 19.   Unanswered questions are referred to senior staff member and/or reference supervisor.

20.   An arrangement is made to call the person back or have him or her call back at a specific time,
[ ]   if a search takes   (20) 2-5 minutes
[ ]   (21) 5-10 minutes
[ ]   (22) 10-15 minutes
[ ]   (23) more than 15 minutes

[ ] 24.   The printed source of the answer is shown to the walk-in inquirer.

[ ] 25.   The source of the answer is cited for the telephone inquirer.

Personnel

[ ] 26.   Personal philosophies and attitudes of reference librarians are not reflected in the execution of service or in the extent and accuracy of information at my library.

[ ] 27.   A professional librarian/information specialist is available to users during hours the library is open.

[ ] 28.   Individual librarians/information specialists have training in specific subject fields.

[ ] 29.   Reference librarians participate in continuing education programs for the librarian/information specialists.

[ ] 30.   Staff members responsible for the delivery of reference/information services are provided with a written job description.

[ ] 31.   Persons not holding the M. L. S. degree serve on the reference desk.

32.   When that happens, they are instructed to answer:

[251]

[ ]   (a) directional questions
[ ]   (b) general questions
[ ]   (c) fact-type questions
[ ]   (d) any reference questions

[ ] 33. Inquiries not answered when they were taken while on desk duty are answered by the person who accepted them unless other arrangements have been made or other demands for the service interfere.

[ ] 34. It is the responsibility of the reference staff member to interview the questioner to determine accurately what information is needed.

[ ] 35. Reference staff members are instructed to follow up on questions to insure that the users' information needs are satisfied.

Reference Collection

[ ] 36. In answering reference questions the whole library collection may be used, not just the reference collection.

[ ] 37. All information materials are examined regularly for currency.

[ ] 38. Frequently used materials are available in multiple copies in order to address user demands more quickly.

[ ] 39. The size (number of volumes) of the reference collection is adequate for answering reference/information questions received from users.

[ ] 40. The currency (up-to-dateness) of the reference collection is adequate for answering reference/information questions received from users.

Thank you for completing the questionnaire. Please use the back of this sheet to make any comments you have about the survey or your library's reference/information services.

[252]

Appendix E

CHILDERS'S SCALE OF CORRECTNESS (SCALE A)
AND ITS CODE*

Scale A   1   0
             (C or P+)   (P- or N or R)

The Code

C = The final answer is wholly correct.

P+ = (a) The correct answer is included in the response, but incorrect information directly related follows or immediately precedes the answer.

(b) The correct answer is given, but is presented in such a way that an inquirer would likely be uncertain that he had gotten the correct answer.

P- = The correct answer is not given, but the response does indicate a substantive step toward the correct answer; that is, part of the correct answer is given.

N = (a) The answer given is wholly incorrect.

(b) No answer is given, but there was some consultation with printed sources or other persons on the part of the respondent.

R = There was no attempt to answer the question correctly. That is, the respondent, without leaving the phone to consult a printed source or another person, indicated that he would not be able to answer the question.

---

*Source: Terence Crowley and Thomas Childers, Information Service in Public Libraries: Two Studies (Metuchen, N.J.: Scarecrow, 1971), pp. 115-17.

Appendix F

STATISTICS DESCRIBING THE FIVE MINOR DEPENDENT VARIABLES

1. Number of Calls:

Mean	1.5	Minimum	1.3
Variance	0.1	Maximum	1.9
Range	0.6	SD	0.2

2. Length of Time per Observation:

Mean	7.2	Minimum	6.5
Variance	0.4	Maximum	7.9
Range	1.4	SD	0.7

3. Sources Volunteered:

Mean	0.6	Minimum	0.5
Variance	0.0	Maximum	0.7
Range	0.2	SD	0.1

4. Attitude:

Mean	1.4	Minimum	1.3
Variance	0.0	Maximum	1.5
Range	0.2	SD	0.1

5. Sex of Respondent:

Mean	34.8	Minimum	8.6
Variance	646.5	Maximum	74.3
Range	65.7	SD	25.4

Appendix G

CORRECT ANSWERS, BY LIBRARY

Library	Number of Questions	Number of Correct Answers	Percentage of Correct Answers
1	35	16	45.7%
2	35	18	51.4%
3	35	22	62.9%
4	35	17	48.6%
5	35	26	74.3%
Total	175	99	Mean: 56.6%

Appendix H

CORRECT ANSWERS, BY QUESTION

Question	Number of Times Questions Asked	Number of Correct Answers	Percentage of Correct Answers
1	5	2	40%
2	5	2	40%
3	5	5	100%
4	5	5	100%
5	5	5	100%
6	5	5	100%
7	5	2	40%
8	5	2	40%
9	5	3	60%
10	5	2	40%
11	5	3	60%
12	5	3	60%
13	5	1	20%
14	5	3	60%
15	5	1	20%
16	5	5	100%
17	5	1	20%
18	5	3	60%
19	5	3	60%
20	5	1	20%
21	5	4	80%
22	5	3	60%
23	5	4	80%
24	5	4	80%
25	5	5	100%
26	5	0	0%
27	5	0	0%
28	5	1	20%
29	5	5	100%
30	5	5	100%
31	5	2	40%
32	5	4	80%
33	5	2	40%
34	5	2	40%
35	5	2	40%
Total	175	99	Mean: 56.6%

NOTES

Chapter 1

1. Terence Crowley and Thomas Childers, Information Service in Public Libraries: Two Studies (Metuchen, N.J.: Scarecrow, 1971).

2. Jassim M. Jirjees, "The Accuracy of Selected Northeastern College Library Reference/Information Telephone Services in Responding to Factual Inquiries" (Ph.D. dissertation, Rutgers University, 1980).

3. Crowley and Childers, p. 171.

4. Ronald R. Powell, "An Investigation of the Relationship Between Reference Collection Size and Other Reference Service Factors and Success in Answering Questions" (Ph.D. dissertation, University of Illinois, 1976).

5. National Center for Education Statistics, Library Statistics of Colleges and Universities 1975 (Washington, D.C.: Government Printing Office, 1977).

6. Norman K. Denzin, The Research Act (New York: McGraw-Hill, 1978), pp. 327-34.

7. J. Sergean, "Correspondence," Library Quarterly 43 (January 1973): 64-65.

8. Denzin, p. 334.

9. H. W. Smith, Strategies of Social Research (Englewood Cliffs, N.J.: Prentice-Hall, 1975), p. 5.

10. "Ethics of Service," RQ 18 (Fall 1978): 57.

Chapter 2

1. Samuel Rothstein, "Measurement and Evaluation of Reference Service," Library Trends 12 (January 1964): 456.

2. Elizabeth O. Stone, "Methods of Evaluating Reference Service," Library Journal 67 (April 1, 1942): 296.

3. Rothstein, p. 464.

4. T. L. Weech, "Evaluation of Adult Reference Service," Library Trends 22 (January 1974): 328.

5. F. W. Lancaster, The Measurement and Evaluation of Library Services (Washington, D.C.: Information Resources Press, 1977).

6. Powell; Charles Bunge, Professional Education and Reference Efficiency (Springfield: Illinois State Library, 1967); Herbert Goldhor, A Plan for the Development of Public Library Service in the Minneapolis-St. Paul Metropolitan Area (Minneapolis: Metropolitan-Library Service Agency, January 1967); Arthur D. Little, Inc., A Plan of Library Service for the Commonwealth of Kentucky: Report to Kentucky Department of Libraries (Cambridge, Massachusetts: Arthur D. Little, Inc., 1969); New York Commissioner of Education, Committee on Public Library Service, Report ... 1957 (Albany: University of the State of New York, 1958); Emerging Library Systems: The 1963-66 Evaluation of the New York State Public Library Systems (Albany: University of the State of New York, 1967).

7. See for example, Marcia J. Myers, "The Effectiveness of Telephone Reference/Information Services in Academic Libraries in the Southeast" (Ph.D. dissertation, Florida State University, 1979), pp. 10-28; Weech, pp. 315-35; and Lancaster, pp. 73-140.

8. Crowley and Childers, pp. 1-84.

9. Lancaster, p. 98.

10. L. A. Martin, Library Response to Urban Change: A

Study of the Chicago Public Library (Chicago: American Library Association, 1969).

11. "Library Reference Service Found Lacking in Test," Library Journal 97 (October 1, 1972): 3110.

12. "Maryland Reference Service Evaluated by Phone," Library Journal 99 (December 15, 1974): 3166.

13. Thomas Childers, The Effectiveness of Information Service in Public Libraries: Suffolk County: Final Report (Philadelphia: School of Library and Information Science, Drexel University, July 1, 1978).

14. Dorman H. Smith, "A Matter of Confidence," Library Journal 97 (April 1, 1972): 1240.

15. Tri-County Regional Planning Commission (Medina-Summit-Portage) and Ralph Blasingame, Survey of Public Libraries: Summit County (Akron, Ohio, 1972).

16. "'Unobtrusive Testing' Used in Ohio Survey," News from the State Library of Ohio, 1974, p. 88.

17. Geraldine King and Rachel Berry, Evaluation of the University of Minnesota Libraries Reference Department Telephone Information Service: Pilot Study (Minneapolis: University of Minnesota, Library School, 1973), p. 58. ERIC Document ED 077 517.

18. Peat, Marwick, Mitchell and Company, California Public Library Systems: A Comprehensive Review with Guidelines for the Next Decade (Los Angeles: Peat, Marwick, Mitchell and Company, 1975).

19. Myers, p. 377.

20. D. E. House, "Reference Efficiency or Reference Deficiency," Library Association Record 76 (November 1974): 222-23; M. J. Ramsden, Performance Measures of Some Public Libraries; A Report to the Library Council of Victoria (Melbourne: Library Council of Victoria, 1978), pp. 51-79; Janine Schmidt, "Evaluation of Reference Service in College Libraries, in New South Wales, Australia," in ALA, LAMA, Library Effectiveness: A State of the Art (Chicago: ALA, 1980), pp. 265-94.

21. House, p. 223.

22. Billy R. Wilkinson, Reference Services for Undergraduate Students: Four Case Studies (Metuchen, N.J.: Scarecrow, 1972), pp. 329-49.

Chapter 3

1. Wilkinson, p. 349.

2. Julian L. Simon, Basic Research Methods in Social Science (New York: Random House, 1969), p. 46.

3. National Center for Education Statistics, Education Directory, Colleges and Universities 1977-78 (Washington, D.C.: Government Printing Office, 1978).

4. National Center for Education Statistics, Library Statistics of Colleges and Universities 1975.

5. Sources of reference questions used in compiling the list of thirty-five test questions included: Bunge; Childers; Crowley and Childers; Myers; Gerald Jahoda and Judith S. Braunagel, The Librarian and Reference Queries: A Systematic Approach (New York: Academic Press, 1980); and Thomas P. Slavens, ed., Informational Interviews and Questions (Metuchen, N.J.: Scarecrow, 1978). The following also supplied questions based on actual contacts with reference departments in their respective institutions: (1) Mary Beilby, SUNY, College at Cortland; (2) Fred Paul Borchuck, Shippensburg State College, Pa.; (3) C. Brightenback, Douglass Library, Rutgers University; (4) David Carr, Alexander Library, Rutgers University; (5) Edsel McCoy, Schomburg Center for Research in Black Culture; and (6) Eric Heubacher, Baruch College Library, New York. Additionally, in order to cover a broader spectrum of disciplines, questions were obtained from experts in areas such as Economics, Education, Biology, Computer Science, Food Science, Engineering, and Philosophy, et al.

6. Powell, p. 34.

7. Frederic M. Lord and Melvin R. Novick, Statistical Theories and Mental Test Scores (Reading, Mass.: Addison-Wesley, 1968), p. 153.

8. Crowley and Childers, p. 28.

9. Florence R. Van Hoesen, "An Analysis of Adult Reference Work in Public Libraries As an Approach to the Content of a Reference Course" (Ph. D. dissertation, University of Chicago, 1948), pp. 207-14.

10. Crowley and Childers, pp. 106-07.

11. Tri-County Regional Planning Commission (Medina-Summit-Portage) and Blasingame, p. 115.

12. Crowley and Childers, p. 34.

13. SPSS, Statistical Package for the Social Sciences, 2d ed. (New York: McGraw-Hill, 1975).

Chapter 4

1. Eugene J. Webb et al., Unobtrusive Measures: Non-Reactive Research in the Social Sciences (Chicago: Rand McNally, 1966), pp. 169-70; Crowley and Childers, p. 120; Myers, p. 84.

Chapter 5

1. M. Johnson and R. Liebert, Statistics Tool of the Behavioral Sciences (Englewood Cliffs, N. J.: Prentice-Hall, 1977), p. 180.

2. John E. Freund, Modern Elementary Statistics, 4th ed. (Englewood Cliffs, N. J.: Prentice-Hall, 1973), p. 306.

3. Alice I. Bryant, The Public Librarian; A Report of the Public Library Inquiry (New York: Columbia University Press, 1952).

Chapter 6

1. Crowley and Childers, p. 47.

2. James Mark Baldwin, Dictionary of Philosophy and Psychology (Massachusetts: P. Smith, 1960), Vol. 2, p. 94.

3. For calculating formula, see Janet T. Spence et al., Elementary Statistics, 2d ed. (New York: Appleton-Century-Crofts, 1968), pp. 216-30.

Chapter 7

1. Myers, p. 286.

2. American Library Association, Reference and Adult Services Division, Standards Committee, "A Commitment to Information Services: Developmental Guidelines," RQ 15 (Summer 1976): 327-29.

3. Thomas Childers, "Managing the Quality of Reference/ Information Service," Library Quarterly 42 (April 1972): 216.

BIBLIOGRAPHY

American Library Association. Reference and Adult Services
    Division. Standards Committee. "A Commitment to
    Information Services: Developmental Guidelines." RQ
    15 (Summer 1976): 327-29.

Childers, Thomas. The Effectiveness of Information Service
    in Public Libraries: Suffolk County: Final Report.
    Philadelphia: School of Library and Information Sci-
    ence, Drexel University, 1978.

_____. "Managing the Quality of Reference/Information
    Service." Library Quarterly 42 (April 1972): 212-17.

Crowley, Terence, and Thomas Childers. Information Serv-
    ice in Public Libraries: Two Studies. Metuchen,
    N.J.: Scarecrow, 1971.

DeProspo, Ernest R.; Ellen Altman; and Kenneth B. Beasley.
    Performance Measures for Public Libraries. Chicago:
    ALA, 1973.

Figueiredo, Nice M. de. "A Conceptual Methodology for Er-
    ror Prevention in Reference Work." Ph.D. disserta-
    tion, Florida State University, 1975.

House, D. E. "Reference Efficiency or Reference Deficiency."
    Library Association Record 76 (November 1974): 222-
    23.

Jahoda, Gerald, and Judith S. Braunagel. The Librarian and
    Reference Queries: A Systematic Approach. New
    York: Academic Press, 1980.

[263]

King, Geraldine B., and Rachel Berry. Evaluation of the University of Minnesota Libraries Reference Department Telephone Information Service: Pilot Study. Minneapolis: University of Minnesota, Library School, 1973. ERIC Document ED 077 517.

Lancaster, F. W. The Measurement and Evaluation of Library Services. Washington, D.C.: Information Resources Press, 1977.

Lynch, Mary Jo. "Academic Library Reference Policy Statements: Toward a Definition of Service." RQ 11 (Spring 1972): 222-26.

Myers, Marcia J. "The Effectiveness of Telephone Reference/Information Services in Academic Libraries in the Southeast." Ph.D. dissertation, Florida State University, 1979.

Peat, Marwick, Mitchell and Company. "California Public Library Systems: A Comprehensive Review with Guidelines for the Next Decade." Los Angeles: Peat, Marwick, Mitchell and Company, 1975. ERIC Document ED 105 906.

Powell, Ronald R. "An Investigation of the Relationship Between Reference Collection Size and Other Reference Service Factors and Success in Answering Reference Questions." Ph.D. dissertation, University of Illinois, 1976.

Ramsden, M. J. Performance Measures of Some Public Libraries; A Report to the Library Council of Victoria. Melbourne, Australia: Library Council of Victoria, 1978.

Rothstein, Samuel. "The Measurement and Evaluation of Reference Service." Library Trends 12 (January 1964): 456-72.

Schmidt, Janine. "Evaluation of Reference Service in College Libraries, in New South Wales, Australia." In Library Effectiveness: A State of the Art, pp. 272-294. Chicago: ALA, 1980.

Webb, Eugene J., et al. Unobtrusive Measures: Nonreactive Research in the Social Sciences. Chicago: Rand McNally, 1966.

Weech, T. L. "Evaluation of Adult Reference Service." Library Trends 22 (January 1974): 315-35.

Wilkinson, Billy R. Reference Services for Undergraduate Students: Four Case Studies. Metuchen, N.J.: Scarecrow, 1972.

INDEX

(Pt. I refers to the Myers study; Pt. II refers to the Jirjees study)

Answers see Questions
Assumptions, Pt. I: 32; Pt. II: 151-152

Berry, R. , Pt. I: 11-12; Pt. II: 164
Blasingame, R. , iv; Pt. II: 146, 163, 259
Bryant, A. , Pt. II: 208

Childers, T. , Pt. I: 9-10, 18, 34, 53-54, 81; Pt. II: 146,
    148, 152-153, 155, 159-163, 169, 172-173, 203, 232-233,
    238, 240-241
Conclusions, Pt. I: 107-109; Pt. II: 234-243
Crowley, T. , Pt. I: 9-10, 55; Pt. II: 146, 148, 152, 159-
    161, 163, 169, 172, 213, 228, 240

Data
    Collection of, Pt. I: 23-28; Pt. II: 180-182
    Treatment of, Pt. I: 28-32; Pt. II: 182-183
Definitions, Pt. I: 15-16; Pt. II: 153-154
Denzin, N. , Pt. II: 155
Dependent variables see Questions--Findings
"Developmental Guidelines" see Reference and Adult Services
    Division--"Developmental Guidelines"
Duncan, C. , Pt. I: 13

Effectiveness see Questions--Findings

267

[268] Index

Ethical issues, Pt. I: 10; Pt. II: 154-156

Figueiredo, N., Pt. I: 109; Pt. II: 236
Financial support, Pt. II: 197, 201, 207

Goldhor, H., Pt. I: 52; Pt. II: 159

Hours open
    Library, Pt. I: 72-78, 80-81, 86-88, 91-96, 106; Pt. II:
        198-201
    Reference, Pt. I: 91-96, 100-102, 107
House, D., Pt. II: 166
Hutchins, M., Pt. I: 8

Independent variables, Pt. I: 25-28, 61-102, 105-107; Pt. II:
    196-208, 238; see also specific independent variables
    such as financial support, hours open, reference--staff,
    resource profile, volumes held

King, G., Pt. I: 11-12; Pt. II: 164

Lancaster, F. W., Pt. I: 7; Pt. II: 158, 160
Lawson, A. V., Pt. I: 12
Limitations
    Of the population, Pt. I: 17-18
    Of the study, Pt. I: 32-33; Pt. II: 154

Martin, L., Pt. I: 7; Pt. II: 161

Ohio Survey, Pt. I: 11; Pt. II: 163-164

Peat, Marwick, Mitchell and Company, Pt. I: 9; Pt. II:
    163-164
Performance see Questions--Findings
Pilot study, Pt. II: 179-180, 184, 235
Powell, R., Pt. I: 10, 97-98; Pt. II: 159

Questionnaires

Construction and application, Pt. I: 25-28, 82-83; Pt. II: 177-179
Findings, Pt. I: 61-102; Pt. II: 188-195
Questions
    Answers, Pt. I: 42-55; Pt. II: 209-227
    Definition, Pt. I: 15; Pt. II: 153
    Findings, Pt. I: 42-62; 104-105; Pt. II: 209-233, 239
    Selection and application, Pt. I: 20-25; Pt. II: 171-182

Ramsden, M. J., Pt. II: 166
Reference
    Information policies, Pt. I: 82-102; Pt. II: 190-208, 238;
        see also Reference and Adult Services Division, "Developmental Guidelines"
    Staff, Pt. I: 83-85, 94-95; Pt. II: 188-190, 196-208, 236-238
Reference and Adult Services Division, "Developmental Guidelines," Pt. I: 5, 85-90, 107; Pt. II: 155, 237
Research
    Design, Pt. I: 16; Pt. II: 170-171
    Hypothesis, Pt. II: 151, 242-243
    Questions, Pt. I: 14-15, 34, 61, 71, 82, 104
    Suggestions for further, Pt. I: 109-110; Pt. II: 242-243
Resource profile, Pt. II: 201-202
Responses see Questions
Rothstein, S., Pt. I: 5, 8; Pt. II: 157-158

Sample
    Of libraries, Pt. I: 18-20, 59-60; Pt. II: 170-171
    Of questions, Pt. I: 19-23; Pt. II: 171-177
Scoring see Data--Treatment of
Sergean, J., Pt. I: 10; Pt. II: 155
Schmidt, J., Pt. II: 166
Simon, J., Pt. II: 170
Smith, D., Pt. II: 163
Smith, H. W., Pt. II: 155
Statistical tests see Data--Treatment of
Stone, E., Pt. II: 157-158
Suffolk County, New York study, Pt. II: 162
Summit County, Ohio study, Pt. II: 163-164

Unobtrusive measures
    Definition, Pt. I: 15
    Findings, Pt. I: 34-42, 104-105; Pt. II: 184-188, 235-236
    Studies, Pt. I: 7-11; Pt. II: 159-167

Van Hoesen, F. , Pt. II: 173
Volumes held
　　Library, Pt. I: 71-79, 86-88, 92-95, 106; Pt. II: 197,
　　　　201
　　Reference, Pt. I: 86-88, 92-100, 107

Webb, E. , Pt. I: 34; Pt. II: 184
Weech, T. , Pt. I: 10; Pt. II: 158
White, R. , Pt. I: 12
Wilkinson, B. , Pt. I: 12; Pt. II: 168-170